COACHING MASTERY

CULTIVATE CONNECTION, EMPOWER YOUR
CLIENTS, AND EXPAND YOUR BUSINESS

TANYA EZEKIEL

Difference Press

Washington, DC, USA

Copyright © Tanya Ezekiel, 2023

All rights reserved. No part of this book may be reproduced in any form without permission in writing from the author. Reviewers may quote brief passages in reviews.

Published 2023

DISCLAIMER

No part of this publication may be reproduced or transmitted in any form or by any means, mechanical or electronic, including photocopying or recording, or by any information storage and retrieval system, or transmitted by email without permission in writing from the author.

Neither the author nor the publisher assumes any responsibility for errors, omissions, or contrary interpretations of the subject matter herein. Any perceived slight of any individual or organization is purely unintentional.

Brand and product names are trademarks or registered trademarks of their respective owners.

Cover Designer: Jennifer Stimson

Editor: Cory Hott

Author photo courtesy of Matt Stokes Photography.

CONTENTS

1. The World Needs More Coaches	1
2. Me	9
3. The Process	21
4. Managing Your Energy and Your Time	29
5. Their Agenda, Your Space	53
6. The Connection Is Magic	69
7. The Department of Corrections	85
8. Endless Possibilities in Co-Creation	97
9. The Coach's Ego	105
10. Money Is Energy	123
11. Sharpen Your Tools	143
12. Is This for You?	149
13. Dream Come True	153
Acknowledgments	159
About the Author	161
About Difference Press	165
Other Books by Difference Press	169
Thank You!	171

For my teacher Benjamin, who saw in me more than I was seeing in myself. He taught me how to take care of people, and modeled loving, courageous, consistent, and transformative relationships with his students. His commitment and passion are endless.

1

THE WORLD NEEDS MORE COACHES

Since the pandemic, there has been an explosion in the coaching industry. From life coaches to business coaches, to relationship coaches, to health coaches, it seems like everywhere you go these days you meet someone who quit their job to become a coach. And the world does need more coaches. We know that coaches get results.

Want to increase your chance of getting a promotion at work? An executive coach increases your chances 2:1 according to Emerald Research.

Want to make sure a patient complies with her doctor's orders? Have them see a coach weekly. The NIH says this will get better outcomes.

Want to decrease athlete burnout? Studies showed implementing effective conflict resolution strategies and improving communication between athlete and coach improved the coach-athlete relationship and increased athletes' perceptions of sport satisfaction.

Want to stop fighting with a loved one? Communication coaching studies indicated coaching intervention reduced total marital burnout as well as physical, mental, and emotional burnout.

Coaching, in fact, does work as numerous studies show. But the efficacy isn't just magic, and with so many new coaches just a year or two into their journeys, we are seeing a lot of coaching novices and not nearly as much coaching mastery as we need. When there is a low bar to entry but high bar to success in an industry, the public gets the impression anybody can do it, but who's actually doing it well?

The need for coaches is on the rise. More and more people are seeking guidance on personal development, work-life balance, career development, and relationships. In addition to the inspiration and tools they need in these areas, they are benefiting from the supportive relationship and space a coach can provide. A recent ICF (International Coaching Federation) survey found that "43 percent of people have used a coach in the past and 22 percent of those who have never used a coach say they are likely to use life coaching in the future."

Jill had hired a coach at a critical transition point in her career and wished she had done so sooner. She was a forty-five-year-old, married mother of two demanding teenagers. After a twenty-year career in pharmaceutical sales, she realized she had nowhere further to go in the organization and she was either going to just stay with it as long as she could hang on or until she burnt out, which wasn't far off. She loved her job, especially the people part. She was good at relating to people and always willing to go above and beyond the sales opportunity to connect them to each other and contribute any way she could, especially to their success. She was surprised how excited she could get about someone else's promotion.

She knew how important mojo was and she loved to lift people up when their careers hit a bump in the road. She had been through a lot of it herself – getting hired, fired, doing the hiring and firing, getting promoted, demoted, winning accounts, losing accounts, you name it. It was nice to be able to leverage her own experiences to help others avoid some of the pain on their journey. People would always say she gave them the best advice.

Three months prior, she had lunch with one of the sales associates on her team who felt a bit defeated in their second year on the job. They were wondering if they were cut out for this work. Jill validated their experience by sharing the moments in her career where she had felt the same, and what tools and perspectives had helped her work through the challenges. Jill walked away from their lunch feeling like she made a meaningful contribution to this person's career and fantasizing about what it would be like to do this every day. It wasn't just at work either. Her neighbor, who was a doctor, needed to talk to somebody who understood the demands and the risks involved in expanding his medical practice. Jill could relate. At first, she hadn't expected her sales experience to translate to medicine, but in that conversation, she realized how much she loved being the person others confided in and how it was so much more about creating a safe space to ask provocative questions than to give answers. Wow, she could get used to this.

And so it began. Her retirement party was on December 15 and within thirty days, she had gone on vacation, started a workout routine, caught up on some sleep and had some precious mommy time with her kids. She was anxious to feel productive again. She posted an update to her LinkedIn page and got lots of likes and a couple of "let's catch up for coffee." Having been in sales, she thought it would be easy to sell coaching sessions.

Nine months had gone by, and she had spent a

lot of time in coffee shops with people saying they wanted to work with her to advance their careers or talking about improving their relationships, but frankly, a surprising number of people ghosted her on the follow-up. She had four people say they wanted a couple of sessions for some guidance. One even agreed to five sessions, paid up front. A couple of them referred friends or partners, but at any given time the most clients she had was five. It was such a range of experiences, not nearly the systematic sales approach she was used to. She always saw herself as a closer but it felt weird to be "closing" people in her network, especially if they were referred to her. She didn't want them to tell their mutual friend that she was being pushy. She was also having a harder time than she expected articulating what they should expect from spending three or six months with her. Not to mention she didn't actually work very long hours but was exhausted!

She read the ICF survey of global coaches, and she charged below the global average because she wanted to see that she could add value first before she charged "full price." She had time set up to meet with her clients, but they always seemed to have something come up last minute, blowing up her plans with rescheduling requests. She had been flexible with her clients since she was a new coach. Logistics aside, when she was with her clients, she was so happy. She loved helping them, she loved solving problems, she loved giving advice. She just wished they'd stick around for more than five to six sessions. She knew so much more was possible for them, but they needed more time together for the magic to unfold.

This could definitely be a full-time career, but she seemed to spend more time trying to build the business than doing the part she loved which is coaching. Plus, the whole money thing felt strange sometimes. "My schedule is at the mercy of other people showing up. It's been twelve months and I feel in many ways that I'm still at square one. Can I make this work? If not, it might be time to find another sales job," she vented to me in desperation.

Does any part of this sound like you? Did you also see yourself as a coach but maybe not as an entrepreneur? Are you also struggling to build momentum in a career you love but just can't figure out where it's not clicking? If so, you are not alone. The same ICF survey Jill was referring to mentioned that the average coach coached six people at a time. That's just not a lot. And that's an average! This presents at least three challenges:

1. How can you get really good at anything if you're not doing enough of it? Didn't Malcolm Gladwell assert in his "10,000-hour rule," that the key to achieving true

expertise in any skill is simply a matter of practicing, albeit in the correct way, for at least 10,000 hours? OK, that's a lot of coaching, and you're unlikely to get anywhere close to being an expert at six sessions a week. If you do the math, however, at twenty sessions a week, you will get there before you know it. I did.

2. If you don't make enough money, you won't be around for long enough to become an expert.
3. If you don't have enough clients, you won't have enough referrals, which will then mean you don't have enough clients to make this career sustainable for you.

Let's remember the world needs more coaches. What if your energy, your passion, your warmth, your kindness, and your determination to contribute to others show you are exactly the coach this world is waiting for? Are you ready?

2

ME

"Insanity is doing the same thing over and over again and expecting different results."

— ALBERT EINSTEIN

In 2010, I turned down a one-million-dollar contract at a global bank and started my career as a coach. Many of my colleagues were hanging onto their Wall Street jobs during the recession, but I just knew leaving was the right thing for me to do. I was certain after just a couple of weeks in the IPEC (Institute for Professional Excellence in Coaching) coach certification program that I had finally found my calling.

It was all coming together.

When I was thirteen, coping with the aftermath

of my parents' divorce, I found answers in the small self-help section at the bookstore at the mall. I continued to be so intrigued with how the brain and the subconscious mind worked that for my sweet sixteen, my friends pitched in and bought me a big book I wanted called *The Mind*. I wanted to become a neuropsychologist, but our family's financial situation led me to pursue a degree with a more direct path to a reliable paycheck, like becoming a teller at the local bank. So I put that curiosity on hold and studied finance. At McGill, where I got my bachelor's degree in international finance, I had space to explore emotional intelligence, culture, and mindset, well before our modern-day definitions of it came; I was chosen to teach the Organizational Behavior Core Course to first-year students while I was in my second year.

Fast forward to the summer of 1996 and I started my career on Wall Street as a bond trader at Salomon Brothers, the best-known bond trading house in the world. I was deep into the thrill and excitement of making money, doing a job I loved, and living life in New York City as a twenty-five-year-old woman. I loved every minute of it. I thought I would be trading bonds for the rest of my life. I never expected my budding teenage interests to come full circle a decade and a half later and bloom into my second career as an entrepreneur and coach.

IPEC's training class was transformative. I remember two specific moments that blew my mind open to what was now possible for me and anyone I came in contact with.

The first was in class during the first training weekend. I was paired up with a woman who was a nurse and wanted to become a coach to help teenage moms through challenging times. I was so moved by her. I had been on Wall Street for fifteen years and while I loved the energy and vibed with the DNA, my peers were not exactly the bleeding-heart types.

Was I?

Here was this beautiful woman, so clear on her mission. She was passionate, driven, warm. I wanted to know more about her and what lessons and experiences contributed to who she had become. When it was time to coach her, I closely followed a couple of scripts on how to acknowledge, validate, and ask an open-ended question, and her eyes filled with tears. I was a bit surprised. I had not spent the past fifteen years moving people to tears, unless we had to report a huge trading loss because Russia's bond market just blew up. Something about her energy, her vulnerability, and her desire to help people opened my heart. I knew this was the career for me.

A few weeks later, we were assigned peer coaches and peer coachees. I was paired with a lovely man who had retired and wanted to get certified as a coach so he could help veterans transition back home. Once again, I was touched by his commitment to others. This was a new world for me. I followed the recommended exercise for the first session which was to have the client rate their level of satisfaction in many different areas of their lives from one to ten, with ten being completely satisfied. Even though I was training to become an executive coach, this approach to coaching the whole person, wherever they were in their life, was new and unexpected.

I was focused on leadership development. Why were we talking about his personal life? It was one of the most valuable and impactful lessons for me. I was surprised to learn how something that appeared to be unrelated to business success, like someone's relationship with a sibling, turned out to unleash so much energy, and ultimately clear the way to increased income. I learned that anything that touched a person's core identity could release or block so much flow. Even though we were working on his relationships with others, he realized how he had allowed others' views of him to affect his most important relationship – with himself. He was due for a realignment.

Back to the life coaching exercise. He rated all categories but one as an eight, nine, or ten. This was a pretty happy guy. He rated "spirituality" a seven. Now you would probably think that's a pretty good score out of ten so carry on. But the difference stuck with me. A week went by, and I kept getting intuitive hits on this seven; I was curious to dig a bit. I technically did a coaching no-no which was to open the session with my question rather than a "how was your week?" and to listen for their agenda. My gut said, "If you feel something, say something," and I just felt it so strongly that I had to ask.

"So, Adam, something stuck with me from our last session, and if you're open to it, I would love to ask a couple of questions around it."

Of course, he said yes with curiosity and enthusiasm. We were both exploring and learning.

"You seem so happy with every area of your life and while seven is still a pretty good level of satisfaction with your spiritual life, it was remarkable that it stood apart from the other areas. What's going on?"

Did I even know what I was asking?

There was silence. I couldn't tell if he didn't have an answer or was contemplating whether he should tell me. I didn't even have much context for my question. I had been studying Kabbalah for a couple of years and was drawn to the system of the Light and the practical application of universal laws and concepts, but it was a far cry from where Adam came from. His response surprised me. "I got divorced a few years ago and was made to leave my catholic church. As a result, I have since lost my connection to God."

Oh boy, what had I gotten myself into? I was taught God is within us and the Light force of Creation is all around us and accessible to us in all ways and at all times. How was I even going to relate to the image he had of God and the power it had over him?

Here's what's truly magical about coaching. It didn't matter what I knew about the Church or God or the Catholic faith myself. I didn't have to teach him what I believed. The only thing that mattered was I had a client in pain, and I wholeheartedly wanted to hold space for him to move through it to a better life for himself. And that we did.

What happened over the next three months was truly miraculous. Everything in his life started changing. It was as if this secret had caused him so much shame and rejection that he was holding himself back from connecting with important people in his life. All his relationships changed, his voice changed, his energy changed, and magically, he even found a church and community who accepted him as he was.

I was onto something. That experience gave me

the awareness that it wasn't what I was coaching him on but who I was being for him and how I was creating a space for his magic to unfold. By having the skills and the courage to cultivate my connection with him and help him go where he had not gone before, with no judgment, I had empowered him. The gift for me, as a coach, was the realization of just how much I could contribute to people's journeys, how much fun I could have doing it, and the knowledge that I could also be successful at it.

CAREER COACH

I knew the network I had built on Wall Street over the prior fifteen years needed some of this magic, and I had to figure out how to bring it to them. People kept asking me "How did you do it? How did you leave such a great career and start all over as an entrepreneur?"

I wasn't even sure but the common theme seemed to be around changes in one's career. I was talking to my friend Fred, who was running the Career Services Office at Cornell's business school. We were exploring launching a leadership coaching program for the graduating MBA class. We defined the different phases of students' careers where they are either looking to a) accelerate their career while staying at or returning to their current role and / or employers, b) transition their career by changing jobs or roles, or c) completely transform their career like I had, to do something totally different.

I knew I could do this for people so I immediately called myself a career coach and it clicked. Everybody needed a career coach.

Imagine a period in life when everywhere you turn, things suddenly show up for you, better than you ever imagined possible. Well, that's what was happening to me. I would bump into people I knew in the street, and they'd want to talk to me about their careers. I would go to dinner with a friend, and they would want to introduce me to a friend going through some changes at work. I would go to a birthday party and come home with three leads and I wasn't even asking for them. All I was saying was "I'm a career coach," to which they all replied, "I need a career coach." and I would say "Come see me. First one's on me." Within three months, I had a full schedule and a list of people waiting for someone to roll off so they could get started.

By some stroke of luck, I searched the URL www.CareerCoach.com and of course it was taken, but I would not settle for that. I hired a web design company and had them hunt down the owner and see if we could pry it away from them. We did. The timing was right for them to cash out on having owned it for many years and it was well worth the investment for me, so I was on my way. Some years later we would rebrand as Conductive for a broader reach. Until then this URL paid off not just by search engines but by the raised eyebrows I got for having the hustle to acquire it.

OFF TO A GOOD START

The URL came after my first few clients were signed up for my career coaching program, which in hindsight was a great thing, and a lesson I want to make sure I pass along here. I saw so many coaches spend months and months branding and rebranding before they approached prospects. They would build websites and design marketing materials, noodling on their niche, and on the name of their company. They would sign up for more coach-training programs, and pay for more business development programs, all while delaying their launch, waiting for perfection.

There is no such thing. This is a person-to-person business, and you don't suddenly become a coach because your website says so. You were always a coach. Think back. When you discovered something exciting, did you share it? When there was a mentor program at your work or community, did you volunteer? Did you always want people you loved to also benefit from a program, a book, a yoga class, an inspiration quote when it did wonders for you? When you're in a good mood, do you want others to be happy? Of course, you do. If all you cared about was your success and privileges, you would not be reading my book.

So here's the story of how I started charging for the thing that I always loved to do and didn't know I could make a business of.

I had this bright idea that I would pick five people and give them ten sessions each as a pilot program and not charge them for it, especially since my certificate was still a couple of months away. I would use our sessions to design the "right" program for people. I told a friend of mine this and she told me about a friend of hers who was looking for a job. I had lunch with this friend, gave her everything I had in the first session, then booked our second, to which she did not show up. I emailed her and she said, "Oh sorry. I took your advice and got a job right away and forgot to tell you." Hmm…

I told my physical therapist that I was doing this pilot and he said he needed help running his fast-growing company so we agreed on a weekly time and place to meet at a coffee shop in the mall across the street from his office. Over the next three weeks I spent anywhere from two hours to four hours waiting for him to be able to take a break from his patients to meet with me. Is this working?

My other friend had been contemplating leaving the asset manager he worked for to start his hedge fund for as long as I could remember. I said, "give me five weeks, let's see what we can create together." Since I wasn't charging him, he spent a few more weeks just contemplating.

That was it. Something was off about this exchange. I turned to both of them and said, "I want to help you, but you don't have enough skin in the game so I'm going to charge you $3,600 for ten sessions and they must be completed within three months."

Well, what do you know? Things started happening for them. Brian launched his hedge fund and Pete grew his practice and later sold it. The amount I asked for just seemed like a price they could pay and was meaningful enough that they would be fully engaged.

I raised my program prices within three months. And then again, and again, and again every few months. By my third year in this business, I was making seven figures and couldn't grow my team fast enough. It wasn't even about the money, but I can tell you if you don't know how to make money in this business it will become about the money, and you will have to throw in the towel at some point. The best way to help a lot of people is to make sure you are creating a sustainable future for yourself and for them.

I will share all my secrets about pricing and raising your prices as you establish yourself, with specific formulas later on in this book. Stay tuned.

3

THE PROCESS

"The process is the purpose."

— MICHAEL BERG

Think about professional athletes. Do they hire fewer coaches as they excel and advance in their careers?

No.

They hire more. They become more aware of the different areas of development at different stages, and they hire a coach for every stage and every challenge. When they have an inquiry, they hire recovery coaches. Then they move leagues, they hire the next level of coach to help them maneuver the move. And when they realize their mental game is off, they hire a coach for that, too.

You see, there is no right or wrong in any of

this. But there is one thing I know to be true, it's that there are not enough successful coaches in this world.

If you are asking yourself why you are not making enough money doing this, I will show you soon. If you are asking yourself why you're so exhausted even though you are doing so well, I will show you why. If you feel you're great with some people and not others or with some situations and not others, I will give you tools to adapt and flow in every situation with every client. First, let's meet my client Russ.

Russ had been a coach for three years when he came to me. He had never made such a meaningful investment in himself or his business but he knew he had to try something different since nothing else had worked. He had written a book, he had become a coach trainer, he had a wide network, and he was active on social media but he just had not cracked it yet.

"I just don't understand why I have not made six figures yet. A lot of people know me as a coach, I get lots of referrals, and many ask to work with me, but it just does not seem to add up. I don't even know if I am charging the right price. Where do I begin?"

I immediately saw that this was going to be a multilevel approach. First, we had to break down his business to see what was and was not working for him. We would have to analyze who he was coaching, where the leads came from, what he was coaching them on, how his programs were structured, and how much he was charging. We would probably have to redesign his offering.

In the process we would discover how he connected with people, and how they connected with him. Was he ready and willing to cultivate deep relationships with his clients to get the results both they and he wanted? Did he have the skills and confidence to empower them? How would he respond if they seemed unsatisfied or were just not making the progress they expected?

He was such a great guy – warm, pleasant, friendly, social, a competitive athlete, and definitely someone you would confide in. He surrounded himself with the right people and knew how to build a network and nurture it. I could even see that from the way he interacted with me. My team always looked forward to his visits to our office.

Did he understand this business is personal? What was less clear in the first meeting was whether he truly understood his role in the relationship. Had he connected the dots yet between his personal development work and the success of his clients? Did he know what filled his tank and what emptied it? Was he trying to fuel other people from an empty tank? His irregular sleep habits were certainly an indication.

By hiring me as his coach, he must have instinctively known he was ready for something different. He was ready for the upgrade that would create greatness for his clients and himself. He borrowed the $10,000 from his dad and we jumped right in.

In Chapter 4 of this book, you will learn how Russ managed his energy first, and his time next. You too will learn how to ask simple questions about who you coach, where you coach them, and how to determine the system that is sustainable for you so that it can be sustainable for your clients. You'll gain insights into your operating model to bring your higher self into the game of coaching.

In Chapter 5, I will share some of my deepest secrets with you about how to create a safe space for your client to flourish in. You will learn an approach that most coaches are not even aware of, which is based on a modern application of ancient wisdom. What you gain from this chapter will drive immediate results for your clients and for yourself.

In Chapter 6, we will then dive into the coaching session's rhythm and dynamics, all of which start well ahead of your meeting with your client.

As we dig deeper, in Chapter 7, into your

personal development as a coach, you will feel like the keys to success are right in your hands. I will teach you the subtle signs you need to look out for to know if, and when, you are losing your mojo and how to recover it quickly.

Chapter 8 will uncover the possibilities for your client, when you tap them into their endless potential. The electricity will flow through you to them, as you ride that wave.

You won't want to miss Chapter 9. There is no doubt your ego will kick in at some point, either to shy you away from what's possible for you as a coach and entrepreneur or to interfere with your momentum in five clearly identifiable ways which I will share with you.

We will talk about money in Chapter 10. If you don't know how to make money as a coach, you won't be making the contribution you were designed for. Can you help the world more with money or without money? So, let's do it. I will show you exactly how I generated over $20 million in coaching revenue.

Russ had some very clear objectives of finding more clients and making more money. He certainly wasn't expecting the depth and breadth we covered in the six months we spent together. He also didn't expect it to have such a long-lasting impact on his life. We caught up recently, ten years since our original work together. It was fun remembering where he came from and seeing just how far he had traveled.

"I have a six-figure business without batting an eye, and working fewer hours than I did back then."

I asked what he remembered from our transformative time together and he shared four main themes:

1. The program was not structured. He was charging by the session and offering half-sessions whenever they wanted it. They called only when they needed guidance urgently, which seemed to serve them – except they were not experiencing lasting changes. He thought he was being accommodating and maintaining a fluid schedule, but he had no consistency or track record as a result. We immediately changed his thirty minutes to sixty minutes and asked for program commitments, paid up front.
2. "You were so open and giving, like letting me use your office for my workshops. It made such a huge difference to me and to my clients. I remember being so surprised by that." He needed a space, I had one available.

To me, it seemed normal. To Russ, it was an example of the generosity of spirit that creates deep and lasting relationships. Why not? Business is personal.

3. "You were good at helping me talk about things I did not want to talk about like my relationship with money. My dad was cheap, and I thought I had to be cheap. As an extension, I also assumed my clients were cheap." Russ's relationship with money was a big topic, as was the importance of understanding value versus price. There were many other things he didn't want to talk about, but for things to really shift, we had to crack them. We tackled his fear of intimacy which was the immediate hunch I had from the thirty-minutes "as needed" sessions he had with his clients. He wasn't looking for a deep connection and his business was suffering as a result.

4. "You taught me to invest in myself. I learned to take care of myself so I would not get burnt out. We created sleep charts together which eventually led me to hiring a sleep coach, and we created a self-care schedule so I could take care of

myself in order to serve others optimally."

As his coach, I will add a fifth here which I remember as a central theme.

When you meet someone who is afraid of being intimate with others, they are also avoiding intimacy with themselves. There's a line we use in coaching that goes, "The way you do one thing is the way you do everything." It refers to patterns. If you don't get close to them, you won't get close to you either. If you don't get close with yourself, then you will *do* coaching, but never *be* the coach people want to get inspired by and stay connected to. This translated into other areas of his life as well.

You are a gift to the world and your desire to contribute to the success of others is exactly what this world needs more of. Now let's get you equipped and fired up and plugged into the circuit of success, happiness, fulfillment, and good fortune for everyone involved.

Are you ready for the ride?

Let's do this.

4

MANAGING YOUR ENERGY AND YOUR TIME

"If you don't know where you are going, any road will lead you there."

— LEWIS CARROLL

Manage your energy, not your time.

In an HBR article with this title from 2007, the authors from The Energy Project wrote, "Defined in physics as the capacity to work, energy comes from four main wellsprings in human beings: the body, emotions, mind, and spirit. In each, energy can be systematically expanded and regularly renewed by establishing specific rituals – behaviors that are intentionally practiced and precisely scheduled, with the goal of making them unconscious and automatic as quickly as possible."

This takes the focus away from time, which is finite, to a renewable source – energy – which is endless. This is done by bringing our awareness to how our operating systems run, and how to create intentional practices to generate energy from our body, emotions, mind, and spirit.

You might be wondering what this has to do with being a successful coach. How would it feel to run a thriving coaching company with more business than you can deliver, with a growing staff, tons of leads, a global presence, making loads of money? What would it take to get there? Energy. It's not all the "hard work, long days" type of energy either. It's the type of energy that is generated from the ease of being in the flow.

Pay close attention here to keeping your tank full. Nothing will derail your business quicker than mismanaging your energy. Have you ever even thought of what fills your tank and what emptied your tank. Try this out. Make a list. Here's mine.

FILLS MY TANK

- Sleeping seven to eight hours per night
- Playing with my kids
- Making social time for friends
- Watching hockey
- White space to create, read, and learn

- Meditating
- Exercising
- Going for a walk
- A big green juice
- My spiritual practice and community

EMPTIES MY TANK

- Drinking alcohol
- Getting into an argument
- Staying indoors all day
- Worrying
- Taking a call from a friend who complains
- Staying out too late
- Back-to-back travel
- Too many distractions
- My iPhone
- Eating crap

WHO, WHAT, WHERE, WHEN, HOW

Now that you're full of beans, let's start with who you will coach. Many coaches decide who they want to coach or don't want to coach and go out looking for those people. If you've been in business for a while, you might already have clear ideas about this, and it may or may not be working for you. With my background in finance, I knew that my greatest contribution would either be to people in finance or those looking to leave and reinvent themselves like I had.

Well, those were not the majority of my first clients in the first year. In fact, it took a few years before 90 percent of my business was in finance. At first, I coached a couple of hedge fund managers and financial services executives, but I also had clients who were in real estate, physical therapy, human resources, politics, consulting, marketing, and even a singer / songwriter. I knew nothing about releasing an album, but I did know how to make things happen through structure, creativity, and accountability. I would sit down with people, listen to their stories about what they wanted to achieve and what they felt was blocking them, and I would detect the gaps in their operating model and lend my skills to them until they had the skills and confidence to do it themselves. I was always transparent about the process because I wanted them to learn how to fish themselves so the changes would benefit them forever, not just while we were together. For example, I didn't tell the artist to just do what I would do. I would have them imagine their way through to completing a task, then I would go back and show them the process that was imbedded in there without their awareness. I always had a knack for pattern-recognition and I enjoyed empowering people with their own ability to recognize their patterns so they could repeat success and get ahead of the downturns in their own performance.

I remember asking the songwriter to talk me through the components of creating her first album and I got up on the board and drew a workflow from the initial spark of a song idea to the release. We would then agree on which steps she could take in the coming week to generate momentum, and she would come back the next week one step closer to making it happen. Of course, along with the logistics and process, I had my senses out for how she was getting in her own way with limiting beliefs or derailing storytelling. I would break those apart in the session as well.

Did I ever think I could coach an artist? Never. By listening to my market as opposed to telling it what I wanted, I learned about my capabilities as a coach, beyond what I could imagine.

Each one of these clients had a pattern. They had a vision of what they wanted to create yet didn't have an executable plan, which meant they did not have the clarity on how to make it happen. They also didn't have the support and accountability. They interpreted this as a lack of confidence.

What is "confidence" really? Confidence is a feeling of trust in your own abilities, and the circumstances. That trust can come from having a plan so you can foresee a trajectory. It can come from remembering prior successes, like knowing you can run 5K in less than thirty minutes because you do it three times a week. It can come from familiar environments in which you know you've been successful before, like playing a team you've won the last eight games against.

You can help your clients gain confidence by being the relationships they can rely on. You can also help build their self-esteem, cheering as well as challenging them, and knowing the right time for either.

Many people came to me or sent people my way saying they needed more confidence. Confidence comes from all the above and from another important ingredient: momentum.

How do you build momentum? One baby step at a time. No matter how small your first goal is, when you achieve it, you want to achieve your second. It's the coach's job to keep those goals small, and executable so it feels so doable and easy for you. In our coaches' training we call them SMART goals: Specific, Measurable, Achievable, Relevant, and Time-bound.

Sometimes, my A-type clients will get frustrated that I am only giving them one little thing to achieve or complete until our next session. We tend to think perfection and overachievement are what drive long-term results, but they create a lot of stop-and-start energy which can be limiting. I just think about it as anything that's going to give you mojo. With mojo, everything seems more achievable for you, and with ease. The other little secret, acknowledging successes no matter how small.

To wrap up, look around for who's attracted to your coaching and why. What do they have in common? What role are you playing for them that you may not have even been aware of? Look for the patterns. If your first ten people are telling you something, then if you turn that into what you tell the next ten people you meet, before you know it, you'll have a special sauce and a thriving business. A win-win for everyone.

You might ask me, "But how does that bring me to my niche?" When you have a steady flow of new clients, you can shape who you take on yourself and who you might pass on to another coach you hire or affiliate with. It is important not to block the flow by your judgment of who a valuable client is. Let them come to you. You will have plenty of time to refine your niche but if you block the flow too soon you will not have anyone to work with. Everyone is coming to you for a reason. Invite them in.

Within nine months of this open-door model, I had to hire four coaches to meet the incoming demand of clients. In the process, I could hand-pick the best fits. For the others, I would close the initial meeting by telling them why I felt this other coach would be perfect for them and most of the time they signed up before even meeting the other coaches.

LOCATION, LOCATION, LOCATION

I'm based in New York City which meant in 2011, I had a good map of where all the Le Pain Quotidien coffee shops were as a perfect place to meet clients. It only took me about a month of loud cafés, constant interruptions, and meetings that started late and ran over before I realized this wasn't for me. This was not the experience I wanted to create for people. As one thing led to another, which often does when you're in flow, an old colleague of mine had suggested I meet a friend of his who was a headhunter and perhaps we could work together. I went to meet him and while I didn't want to become a headhunter, I thought our business opportunities could align and I liked his office. I saw that he had an empty desk and beautiful meeting room so I asked to move in.

It was amazing. I was in the heart of Manhattan, at 11 East 44th, right outside Grand Central – an excellent location for anyone coming from around the city or from outside. We shared the open space, and I used this beautiful meeting room with a large glass table for one-on-one client meetings as well as team meetings for up to six people. This happened only a month after I started my business, and I ended up staying there for a couple of years before I moved upstairs in the same building to have room to build my team.

The dynamic with my clients totally changed from the café rendezvous. I started defining how I wanted my clients to feel when they came in for a session, and not just what they received as an outcome from the session. The referrals were nonstop. I couldn't keep up. I had a model of how many business development meetings I needed each week to maintain the number of client sessions I wanted to deliver each week and the intensity was high. I was working eighty-hour weeks and loving every minute and never feeling tired. More about this later.

HOW MUCH IS ENOUGH

While it may not feel like this is your problem right now, if you follow everything I offer you in this book, it will be sooner than you think.

Let's say you left your full-time job, and you are all-in and have your entrepreneur's hat on to build an awesome business. Your heart is on your sleeve to help as many people as you can. Here's how the formula works.

If you're just getting started, you will need about two hours to support every hour of coaching. This means that if you want fifteen clients each week, you will probably be putting in forty-five hours a week. I bet you're surprised at that number. In the thirty hours beyond your sessions, you are emailing, scheduling, learning, taking notes, reading notes, researching industries and job functions to better understand your clients, meeting new prospects, meetings friends who might lead you to new prospects, more scheduling and rescheduling, putting in place new systems, infrastructure, tracking spreadsheets, maybe even a CRM, talking to accountants, lawyers, web designers, hiring your own coaches and watching their videos, and listening to their advice, and so on, and so on. Get it?

In the first three months, I was fully booked at twenty-five client sessions each week, five lunches or coffees for new business, and I had a waitlist of people wanting to get started. If you do the math, that's how I was at work at least 7:00 a.m. to 8:00 p.m. each day and doing some cleanup on the weekends. Oh, was it fun!

Over time, as your administrative team grows, you may only need one hour to support each client session. My target for new coach hires was for them to deliver twenty coaching sessions per week, which was easily a fifty-hour week and then some, even though we had five team members supporting us.

As an entrepreneur, it is critical that you are modeling your business for sustainability. It will not be possible to maintain a small number of clients, which is why part-time coaches do not really succeed. Would you go to a part-time dentist for a root canal? Why would you trust your career or your life's journey to a part-time coach. You probably would not. So either your number of active clients will go to twenty or thirty with an average of twenty to twenty-five sessions per week because you're rockin' it, or it will go to zero because you never built the momentum you needed for long-term growth

The key questions you want to ask yourself right now are:

1. Am I all-in?
2. How many hours do I want to work each week?
3. Am I ready to show up to work each day as if it's a "job"?

Listen, I don't want you to feel like this is a job, but I can tell you this is the best job in the world. You go to work each day helping others succeed and go home each night fulfilled and aligned with your soul's purpose. Contributing to other people's success is a gift.

After many years at this rhythm, I was able to build a strong team, and together we delivered over 2500 coaching sessions each year. When you reach this kind of business momentum, you can then go through some seasons where you can choose to take your foot off the pedal for a period of time and coach half as many clients. You will be able to turn it up and dial it down any time because your brand and reputation are known and the number of people who have experience with your company will be great enough to keep the flow going for many years to come. To have this level of flexibility, you will need a period of strong and sustainable growth up-front. If you enter this business for flexibility up-front, you will be limiting your options too soon.

I HAVE A SYSTEM AND IT WORKS

I had a system and it worked. Meetings took place in my office, not theirs. At the beginning, I had a three-month program which was to be paid for up front before the first session. It wasn't a three-month program with monthly payments because that's just a monthly program with an option to continue. The way I worked, clients felt pretty good in week three but the real changes needed the eight to ten sessions to take place. There's a fair bit of experimentation that takes place in the first three months to see what approaches and techniques really make this particular client tick. So, unless they committed to another three or six months, the new behaviors did not always become habitual and sustainable. Something to think about as you design your programs. Over time, you will have the confidence to require a minimum six-month commitment.

I met Gary at a talk Thomas Friedman was giving at a consulting company. I could immediately tell he was funny and made friends easily. Just as I was leaving, he and his wife started chatting with me and he asked what I do, and I said, "I'm a career coach," to which he replied to the exact thing almost anyone I said that to did. "Oh, I could use a career coach." I coached Gary through a couple of career transitions, including the launch of his start-up. I would not have expected Gary to be my "ideal" client since he had a background in politics rather than finance, but we had a great connection, he was very committed to the process, and he loved referring people to me. Remember how I said don't judge your clients for whether they fit your imagined niche. Observe and learn from your audience.

Gary had this gift of connecting with interesting, ambitious people who were often at the leading edge of change so I was always excited to meet his friends, like Nicole.

Nicole had written a book and was looking to take her career, brand, and platform to the next level. She signed up on the spot. In my enthusiasm to be of service to her, I got a little more flexible with my system than I normally would. When people couldn't make it into my office, I would offer them a phone session (pre-Zoom times). In her case she wanted to meet in person and came to my office a couple of times, but then said she was too busy to travel to my office. Against my better judgment, I agreed to travel to her, and we met in a restaurant near her home.

Let me interrupt this story for a bit of business math. I was scheduled back-to-back because I enjoyed my client meetings so much that I wasn't efficient at ending my sessions on time unless someone else was waiting and even if I did, I couldn't get much work done in a small break. It was therefore easier for me to have a 12:00 p.m., 1:00 p.m., 2:00 p.m., 3:00 p.m., etcetera. So, to go meet her for lunch at 1:00 p.m., I had to use the 12:00 p.m., 1:00 p.m., and 2:00 p.m. spots. Now that may not seem like a big deal, but it was not the system that had been working for me.

We met over lunch near her home and her tone was quite different, more casual, more friendly, with a bit more venting, less eager to learn, and slightly less engaged. It was harder to get her focused on the objectives we had set out for the engagement, and she just didn't seem as receptive. We did this three times before she felt she wasn't getting as much as she had expected out of the coaching. I had a system, and it worked. Deviating from the system did not. She stopped scheduling and a few months later she asked if she could donate her remaining sessions to a friend and we did.

Another similar situation happened with a friend who wanted to pay in installments. Of course, he was a dear friend, how could I say no? After four weeks, something came up and he had to use the money for a project which seemed to him more urgent. We had just gotten to breaking down all the areas of his business that needed to be upgraded and tackling a couple of time-sensitive issues with staffing and accounting. Four weeks was just not enough time for the coaching to be transformative, especially with so many fires to put out.

I also never barter. Here's why. For example, coaches will coach their personal trainers in exchange for training sessions. So I had a client who was an interior designer and I needed some help with my new office. He insisted we swap. It seemed like a good idea to fill both of our needs without an exchange in cash. Before I knew it, he started arguing that what he had designed for me was beyond the scope he intended and that his rate for this would exceed our swap and that I owed him money. It came apart pretty quickly. We probably could have made it work if we both wrote contracts up front, agreed to the deliverables and then netted out the difference but is this the type of negotiation you want to enter in with a coaching client? I, of course, developed close relationships with my clients and trusted their work but was he really the designer I would have hired if I were going to pay for it? I certainly couldn't have said that either. Not a win-win situation. I never did it again. From that point forward it was, "I pay your fee, you pay mine" or we just give each other advice as friends but no formal swaps.

OK, one more. In 2011, in my third month coaching, a client came to me hesitant to sign up for my then three-month program at $5,000 for ten sessions. She said she just wanted help with her resume. I told her resume reviews happen as part of the process when needed but that I wouldn't do a one-off resume review. I would, however, be happy to meet with her for a chemistry meeting and if it felt right to both of us then she could sign up for my program. Nope, she wouldn't have it. She insisted on paying me for that session because she needed her resume reviewed. I gave in, hoping I could convert her into a client after the session.

I treat resumes as a branding and marketing product so first I have to get a sense of who you are and how you operate and regardless of what you've done for work, I want to feel that your real persona and operating model are coming through this *one* page of paper. So we spent the first twenty minutes or so going through her story then getting tactical. After sixty minutes, I wasn't sure if I had given her enough value, so I kept going for another half hour (red alert!). She paid me the $500 and decided not to continue working with me. Was every session always worth $500? I don't know, but I did know for sure that ten sessions were always a higher ROI (return on investment) than $5,000.

I knew I had broken my "first one's on me" system so I consulted my business development coach Julie Steelman (author of *Effortless Yes*) and she confirmed by saying "Give a session, get a client." Ohhh. Such good advice. I never did that again.

These systems work for me. You will find the ones that work for you. When you do, stick to them and question what agenda you have for going out of your way and risking what you know works for you. Are you trying to prove something? Are you looking for approval? How is this serving you or your client?

COACHING FRIENDS

I get this question a lot and I hear black-and-white positions on coaching friends. Mine was always that if you are in this business to help people, why would you not want to create magic for people you care for the most? I have coached many friends, and, in all cases, it brought us closer. Sometimes a friend will ask to be coached through something, in exchange for which I always accept sushi and tequila. I am so grateful for the gifts I have been given to be able to contribute to others' success. I would never hold that back from those who matter most to me. They do gain insights from our lunch but if they want real change, I make it clear they need to be in a coaching program, for the entire engagement, almost weekly meetings, paid up front. The system does work. Then we can do the deep dives, I can hold them accountable, and the real transformation takes place.

I know I have given you a lot to work on and we are not even halfway there but stay with me. This is not a game of perfection. This is a people business, and you are human as well. You will cycle through your own seasons and go through your own changes along the way. Be patient with yourself, manage your energy and manage your time. In order to manage your time, you must manage your energy. I have a rigorous time management system with color blocks and categories. If you want access to it, you can reach out to me and I can send you a webinar where I taught it.

The bottom line is if it's not on my calendar then it's not happening. When I'm feeling energized and ambitious, I spend a great amount of time proactively managing my calendar, then I just react to whatever it tells me to do. I honor my productivity cycles. I learned an amazing productivity tip from my dear friend, and coach extraordinaire Taki Moore. I plan a demanding six-week cycle of creativity and follow it diligently. Then I need a little break of one to two weeks to flow more freely where I want to generate something new and give myself some creative space. In the six-week cycle, my calendar will be color blocked from 6:00 a.m. to 10:00 p.m. I feel like I'm firing on all cylinders. I'm working out five times per week, I'm eating clean, sleeping well, seeing tons of clients, and overall feeling awesome. At the end of the cycle, I take a week or two to revise the schedule template for the next six-week cycle and give myself some time and space to reimagine life and living. I might give myself a break to go on a retreat or training event to refuel the tank as well.

BE VERSUS DO

In *Letting Go*, David R. Hawkins wrote that the basis of our value and how others rate us has been based on what we *do* in the world. He said, "As we move up in lovingness, our *doingness* is less and less preoccupied with self-service and becomes more and more oriented toward others. As our consciousness grows, we see that service, which is lovingly oriented toward others, automatically results in the fulfillment of our own needs. [...] At that point it is no long what we *do* in the world but what we *are* that counts."

Ana called me and I could hear the frustration and, dare I say, self-judgment, in her voice. "I have a growing list of things I need to do for myself, my kids, my husband, our cafe. I have things I need to schedule for my students, and other people I'm responsible for. Every day I look at this list and I feel like I'm not getting things done. I have tried to take your advice to work with time blocks but then I don't have the discipline to follow the plan. Some things do get done, but other things just keep getting rolled over. I don't know any other technique except checking off the easy things first. Help. What can I do? I don't ask because I think it's a stupid question but how do you get things done? You prioritize and just follow through, right? I look back on the day and realize I'm constantly busy-busy doing something but it feels like I am not making any progress. Will this to-do list ever be done?"

Ana is a brilliant teacher as well as a mom of three kids, and an entrepreneur. Can you relate to her stress? This was our exchange:

> Me: "Time management is never about time. What would you create if you didn't use time as an excuse?"
>
> Ana: "I would lead much more, connect with more people, create more business."
>
> Me: "What do you get out of avoiding that?"
>
> Ana: "I don't know. I guess I'm afraid, but of what?"
>
> Me: "Without this deep questioning, you can't stick to a schedule because you are asking the outside world to tell you what your priorities are. Your priorities come from who you see yourself to *be*, not what you see yourself *doing*. In the meantime, look at the next six weeks, nothing longer. Who are you in the next six weeks? The who determines the what, Not the other way around."

Ana: "Cool, I need to read this another twenty times and let it sink in."

I gave Ana a lot to think about and I get questions about time management a lot. For you, the question is: "Am I a coach?" Or is this your side gig? You will get back whatever you align with.

You see, I'm never not a coach. I'm a coach in session, I'm a coach at a party, I'm a coach on vacation. It's not that I'm doing the work of coaching all the time, but I identify with the role of a coach 24 / 7. If a friend texts me for advice at 10:00 p.m., I always answer from my higher coach self. This capacity is the greatest gift I've been given. I never shelve it.

This helps me manage my time in alignment with this identity. It's like being a mom. It's my identity. I'm always a mom, wherever I am, whatever I'm doing. I am not always with my kids, but I am always a mom. Because of this, I can easily get coaching tasks and mom tasks off my to-do list because they're not things I *do*; it's who I *be*. With no judgment.

To tie this together, when what I'm doing aligns with my core identity, my tank fills up. Authenticity is a fuel. The best advice I can give you as an entrepreneur is to recognize your patterns, learn your rhythm, and know how to keep your engine running. There are times you will be designing and building systems for yourself and your clients, and there are times you will be just flowing along, in the moment. No system will work forever. You are dynamic and so are your productivity frameworks. Think of them as seasons. Some seasons you will plan the crop and other seasons you will pick the fruit, and each harvest is unique.

Keep your tank full. You can't contribute to others if you are running on empty.

5

THEIR AGENDA, YOUR SPACE

THE "SPACE" VERSUS THE "SPACE"

When a client puts their trust in you, they are putting themselves in a position of receiving guidance, love, support, and many more gifts from you. Receiving is hard. They have to trust someone. Be that someone for them. Make it easy for them to receive from you. There are many components to create this opportunity for your client. We covered some of them in Chapter 4 including having a system that works and staying true to it. We talked about having a physical location that aligns with the dynamic and the experience you desire to create for your client. To be clear, you may decide that physical location is a booth at your favorite diner. If you do that, you will want to make sure you carefully manage some of the variables like what is ordered, when, how, and that you are treating the wait staff as part of your team to create that experience. It is certainly possible. The point here is that it is your responsibility to create that space, physically.

More importantly, and certainly not one without the other, it is also your responsibility to create the Space. Here the capital S refers to the energetic space you are creating. When a client hires you to work with them, they have an agenda, they have intentions and objectives, or at the least they have a strong connection with you and know that you can contribute to their winning outcome and together you create the agenda which will get them there. It is the client's agenda, but it is your Space. The many coaches I have trained have said this was one of the most important lessons they learned from me. This means that you could even be in their office space, but when you are in session, it is your Space. It is your job to create the environment for the transfer of energy between coach and client and to help the client feel safe and assured to receive from you.

You will certainly run into resistance from time to time and the first question you have to ask yourself is, "What can I do or be for this client to receive from me with total ease?" Then energetically lower your walls and barriers to not meet their resistance but disarm it.

Try this with me. Take a deep breath into your belly as you're reading this and imagine you had a little fence all around your body. Now slowly lower it and let it slip into the ground around you. Even lowering your walls is part of the coaching process. So if and when you do run into their walls, no worries at all. It is all part of the process. It is actually very helpful to know where their lines are drawn so you can help them recognize and manage their boundaries in healthy ways. Sometimes I just calmly say "okay" and continue listening. As easy as that. Here's an example:

> Me: "It feels to me like this is a real trigger for you. What do you think is going on here?"

> Client: "I'm not triggered. It's just not right that they sent that email and I don't see how you would think this is my fault."

Yes, this can happen. To make some real shifts you are going to get close to some yuck-and-stuck material. Here's a client who likely has a self-blame default which is not something that you created, nor will you change with one coaching question alone, no matter how brilliant. So you make a mental note to look out for an "it's my fault" pattern and lower your walls and barriers and breathe deeply into your belly and soften your eyes and shoulders so they know you are still with them, and you are still holding the Space for whatever reaction they are having and that nothing scares you. They're just having a moment. It's OK. If you remember that it's your Space and do as I just said, you will see the client match your energy by dropping their shoulders and you'll be able to go deeper.

Here's what losing the Space looks like.

Me: "It feels to me like this is a real trigger for you. What do you think is going on here?"

Client: "I'm not triggered. It's just not right that they sent that email and I don't see how you would think this is my fault."

Me: "I didn't say it's your fault, I just said you seem triggered."

More than the words, it is energetically accompanied with the thoughts of "oh no, I shouldn't have said that, now I got them worked up, we have twenty minutes left to the session, how am I going to turn this around, it's only our third session, what if they ask for their money back and tell my other client who referred them that this was a bad idea?"

You just handed over the keys to your client, and now they feel lost and confused because they weren't planning on driving today. This is also likely followed by an email the week after, two hours before the next session: "Hey, my boss needs something done by tomorrow so I can't make it today. Let's reschedule."

Listen, Coach, you were right, they were triggered, and your question was the right one. The only difference between the two scenarios is you put up a wall when they reacted and gave up the space, leading your client to not feel safe. They may believe everything is their fault, and now they even feel like they offended you. To make matters worse, they don't know how to get out of it because it's not their responsibility to make you feel better about your coaching skills.

ROMEMUT

This brings me to an important concept which has no English translation so bear with me here. It's a word my Kabbalah teacher taught me. It's a combination of awe, respect, and inspiration. Your client must have "romemut" *for* you to receive *from* you. Guess whose responsibility it is to create their romemut for you? Yours. In the example above, you can address the situation and the reaction but never give up the Space because if you do, you are hurting your client's ability to receive from you and that's just not cool.

So let's continue in the above example:

> Me: "I am sorry. I can see that we hit a nerve. It's normal that you would feel this way especially given how hard you have been working on this project and how important it is for you to see every box checked before the deadline. What did this email mean to you?"

There you go. Back on track. You weren't fazed, you are still holding the Space, you are still in session, the client doesn't feel badly for snapping at you, and you have indicated you clearly remain committed to working through this with them. Your client will likely drop their shoulders and take a breath and something else will come up. Look for the breakthrough!

> Client: "I'm exhausted. I haven't taken a day off in three weeks and nobody appreciates how hard I'm working."

Good job, Coach. You stayed in your heart and kept the keys. You also did not lose your position with the client. You did not make it about you. You are here for them and have allowance for their experiences.

The other aspect that contributes to romemut is credibility. For example, you get in front of a new client, and you are a confident and successful coach. You do not feel the need to go over your resume to market yourself, so you say nothing. At the same time some of your clients may want to see that you have what it takes to guide them. They may need to see you as an expert in order to be open to receiving from you. Do not mistake this with your ego. It is important for you to tell them what they need to hear about your skills, experience, and qualifications for their sake and for the sake of them receiving from you.

If it were coming from your ego, you would tell them all that for your sake not theirs. Imagine pouring water from a pitcher into a glass. The pitcher has to be slightly above the glass for the glass to receive water from the pitcher. This is important for your client. I am not saying you're greater than them or better than them. That's irrelevant. What I am saying is you need to be just 10 percent ahead of them in whatever experience they're having, hold the Space, and have the certainty that something magical can happen at any time and you will be there for them when it does, even if you must work through some muck first.

Watch out. You may have a need for approval and validation and one of the ways you get that is by wanting your client to like you right out of the gate. The client may enjoy your company, but the riches of your contributions won't have space to flow from you to them. Your client or prospect will leave the meeting feeling like you're a good person and you will feel good about the connection, but it will be a missed opportunity for both of you. This is your responsibility to sense how the client needs to perceive you in order to engage in a receiving relationship with you and it is your job to maintain that throughout the coaching engagement. If you are listening intuitively, you will pick up on their relationship values, which will come in handy later.

TIME OUT

Time out is another important tool to bring the Space back to you if you feel it might have slipped away. Let's say the last session didn't end as warmly as usual and you felt the client lost a bit of romemut for you. You were feeling a bit insecure and you gave up the Space. Here is how you recover in the next session:

Coach: "I have been thinking about you since our last session together and want to take a little time out to realign with you. How are we doing?" (You can even motion the "you and I" as the "we.")

It doesn't matter where it goes from here. Give them a chance to respond and just coach around whatever comes up. The most important thing is you showed that you weren't put off, nor were you concerned, nor has your commitment to them waivered. The courage you display in holding the Space for your relationship with them will already be just what they needed. Whatever their response to this is, remember you are listening to what they are *not* saying. You are listening for what values they need acknowledged so they are not focusing on the wrongness of them but rather recognizing that what they were looking for was a validation of what matters to them. They may respond:

Client: "I felt like you were judging me for not getting that job."

Coach: "Thank you for sharing that with me. I can see how it came across that way, especially as I did get a little excited about the opportunity. I will be more aware of that. What feels right as a next step in the interview process for you now?"

It takes a lot of courage to be a great coach. There's no right or wrong, only presence. You got this.

DON'T GET IN THE BOX

It can be so tempting to jump in there and say, "I can't believe they sent that email. Clearly they're not on your side." You might even think that, but it does not matter. The most important question you want to be asking yourself and your client, if appropriate, is "Hmm, what's going on here?" Create Space for infinite possibilities and have the knowing that you're not even aware of them all. Notice I said knowing and not knowledge. There is a big difference. Knowledge is the information you have gained to provide some guidance or answers. Knowing is the certainty and intuitive wisdom you have deep inside you that things will work out as they are meant to. There are infinite possibilities available, and you want to guide your client to create more options for themselves and feel empowered and confident to choose.

What if this turned out to be better than they ever imagined possible? Your client may not be ready to hear this. Just saying it in your head and raising your eyebrows with curiosity to see what could possibly unfold next can create magic for them. You are powerful, Coach, especially when you're not saying anything. Imagine that? If you narrow in on solutions and answers, you can block the flow and get into intellectual problem-solving which only works sometimes. If you stay in the question, the Space will remain open for limitless possibilities.

SHALL WE TALK ABOUT YOUR EYEBROWS?

My client Bernard loves this one. He says two of the most valuable things he learned from me are a) the eyebrows (Huh?) and b) that you are only one person and you go everywhere as one. You're not one person at home, another at work, another at the gym. If you are, we might have to get you a different book to read. This is about being all of you, all at once, in all environments. Wow.

Now back to the eyebrows. Time for another experiment. Ask this question:

"Why did your team do that?"

Now try it again. Drop your eyebrows into a deep frown and ask:

"Why did your team do that?"

How do you feel? How does your client feel?

One more time. This time raise your eyebrows

like you just saw something joyfully surprising. I'm exaggerating a bit but work with me.

"Why did your team do that?"

Feel the difference? You can almost smile. I think you would agree the first one feels judgmental and limited. The energy contracts and people immediately feel like they need to defend themselves. In fact, we have learned in coaching school to avoid Why questions altogether. I would add, unless you can raise your eyebrows. A question asked with raised eyebrows shows curiosity. Not much beats curiosity. It has a feeling of: "Wow? Why did the team do that? What result were they looking for? That's so interesting how that happened. Tell me more."

This is especially important when you are talking to yourself.

Lowered eyebrows: "Why did I just do that?" (i.e., "I'm an idiot.")

Raised eyebrows: "Why did I just do that?" (i.e., "Wow. That's wild, I just poured cream into my cup of orange juice.")

So if you see the shadow of your eyebrows when you are asking questions, know the energy you are sending is restrictive, limited, and potentially judgmental. In fact, if your client gets defensive, this is a sign that they feel judged. Just raise your eyebrows and get curious. The same questions will lead to new potentials.

STATE, STORY, STRATEGY

This part applies to you and to your client. Tony Robbins, one of the greatest coaches of our time, talks about this formula of "state, story, and strategy."

The idea is that many people go about looking to change some circumstances in their life by finding a strategy that will work, like getting into shape, finding a new job, or starting a family, etcetera. However, for a strategy to work, you must be telling yourself the right stories, and for you to be able to change those stories if they are not working for you, you need to be in the right State.

Let's keep this simple since almost all of us have tried to get into better shape at some point.

A friend of yours lost thirty pounds on a Keto diet and sends you a list of exactly what to eat and when to eat it. You look at the list, and it seems pretty reasonable for you but immediately the familiar voice in your head pops up: "Ha! Another $400 down the drain for groceries and you know you won't last three days on this. You'll never give up your waffles and bananas for breakfast. Plus, your parents were never able to lose weight so it's in your DNA. You'll never be slim."

You have heard about limiting beliefs and you wonder if you should be thinking more "positively" about this so you try to tell yourself: "This time could be different. Believe in yourself." It's just not sticking. Plus, you haven't slept more than four hours a night all week and you've barely seen daylight. Your beautiful screensaver is as close as you've gotten to a sunrise in two weeks." You are in no state to be able to change your story, so that this Strategy could work for you.

Get it? Change your state, change your story, use the strategy. You got it.

Now back to coaching. My client Bill was obviously brilliant and diligent. He came to our first meeting focused, and ready to do the work. He was particularly bothered by some organizational changes that took place in his company. In his job, he had to influence a broader set of people he had no authority over, and direct members of his team who were not pulling their weight. He felt fingers were pointing at him and he was under a lot of stress. His family felt it too and he was irritable at home. He was excited his boss hired a leadership coach for him and was ready to learn new ways to communicate and organize himself to be more effective.

A couple of weeks into our work I could feel the lethargy. I could feel he was in a state of defeat. I asked what he was doing to take care of himself and the list was short. He reads, he said. I asked about exercise. He said he used to run. He couldn't see how he could fit it into his schedule now, but he'd think about it. I challenged him to run just one mile from his place. The next morning I woke up to a text from him with a picture of the sunrise a mile from his house. He continued running almost every day throughout our engagement. His state shifted and the stories he told himself about everything being out of control melted away. There were certainly circumstances outside his control but his interaction with them changed. He was more matter-of-fact about what he could influence versus what he could not. We created strategies for how he organized and communicated his project priorities and updates to management. He showed up in meetings with a stronger voice and more executive presence. The point is we couldn't put the cart before the horse. He had to be in a "yes I can, yes I can" state, with new stories before we could implement any new strategies.

This applies to you as well, Coach. As with everything else, if you don't follow this formula, you won't inspire others to. You see we cannot make choices for other people but we can make choices for ourselves and inspire others. I have this post-it note on my desk:

"Choose for yourself. Inspire others."

So if you find that you are making plans you don't follow, you're reading mindset strategies that aren't changing the voice in your head, then go back to basics. Remember the list of what fills your tank and what empties your tank in Chapter 4? Go fill your tank and change your state, then everything will get easier for you and the greatest gift of all is that you will be in Flow for your sessions.

I remember when I first started coaching and I needed to make some big decisions about branding, marketing, pricing, business development strategy. I would do a juice fast for three days and the creativity would be explosive and everything seemed possible. Once I saw the impact it had on the way I thought, then I learned to do it more efficiently, like drinking black coffee with MCT oil for the first few hours of the day to start the day with extra energy and creativity. My dear friend MaryRuth Ghiyam published a brilliant book *Liquids Till Lunch* which completely changed the way I eat around my work schedule and the hours and days I want to be most productive.

All this brings us back to you being responsible for the Space you create for your client. How you manage yourself is key to your clients' success. If you want to help others succeed you have to always be willing to do the work yourself. You might even find that when you are driven by being an inspiration to others, amazing things will happen in your life too. It's a win-win.

6

THE CONNECTION IS MAGIC

I knew it from our first meeting in my office. I could usually tell if there was energetic alignment between me and my prospective client from the first contact. It would feel like someone was sent to me rather than I went looking for them. Selena was exactly that. She was poised and professional, but also warm, with a twinkle in her eye. I could feel her inner strength and that she had strong intuition, knowing when something or someone felt right for her. She was thoughtful and not reactive, and I could tell she was concealing her real strength, which was profound. I also knew I was skilled at bringing exactly this type of potential out of people. She felt a bit stuck in her current role, especially as the boss she loved was leaving. There were a lot of logical reasons she wanted a coach, but the real magic was beyond what met the eye on our first meeting. I could not wait to work with her.

Your connection with your client starts before your first meeting. Imagine you've been waiting years to meet each other, and the universe finally aligned your stars for your paths to cross. Your client was assigned to you. Accept the assignment and open your heart and mind to allow the magic to unfold.

Some of you will ask me how I know any of this to be true. Does it matter? What if you received your client in this way whether you believe in universal assignments or not. What state of being would this put you in to be fully present with your client and ready to contribute to their lives? Sometimes coaches show up with all the tools and tips and tricks yet forget that the most important piece of the puzzle is their openness to receive the client and the assignment. You see, you are teaching your client to receive and the best way they learn from you is by mirroring you, even unconsciously.

It is not as much about what you *do* for your client as it is about who you *be* for them. When you approach them with an open heart and mind, they learn to be that for others. When they learn to receive from you, it will put them in a receiving state for all that life has to offer them. You will see that their connection with you can show them how to be in a relationship with others, with money, with their body, with success. Anything is possible.

The coach and coachee (client) synergy can create something from nothing. When there is chemistry, things can move quickly. I am sure you have noticed that some meetings with your clients fly by, and little sparks can quickly turn into a flame and your client is off to the races, feeling confident and energized, ready for action. Yet other times, you may feel you have the best idea for them, and it can fall flat or be met with resistance. All of these are normal, and we all experience them at different times. Remember, it's your Space so let's make sure you have the tools and the mindset to optimize results for your clients.

Let's look at your connection with the client in three phases: before the meeting, during the meeting, and after the meeting.

PRE-MEETING

Whether you have been coaching for many years, or just getting started, treat this as a reset and see if you can take a step back and create some space around your sessions for exploration and insights. There have been many years in my practice where I just went back-to-back all day and had less time to process and download insights between meetings, which meant insights would come to me in the middle of the night, or walking to work, or taking the subway. These were all valuable, yet I was not leaving enough space for creativity. Sometimes you need the intentional space, and other times you don't. Stay aware. At times when I was much firmer with my schedule, I deliberately created space for my mind to "wander" off about my clients and receive fresh insights and perspectives. I want to show you how to receive those as well.

There is a difference between a thought and an insight. We all have intuition and access to greater levels of consciousness than we could ever imagine. How we recognize or interpret the messages is unique to each of us. I will bet, however, that none of us are nearly as in-tune as we can be. Some of us feel, some of us hear, some of us see and most of us don't think we can do any of that. We think we are just thinking.

If you are ready to master your coaching skills, this is an area of growth that will make a significant impact on the results clients get out of your coaching relationship.

You will get efficient over time and will not require the full prep but let's lay it out here as if you have plenty of time right ahead of the session.

1. Close your eyes and as you did before, imagine there may be walls and barriers around you and ask them to lower, as if you just hit a button, and down they went. This will open the flow to give and receive energy.
2. Receive the assignment and the relationship. This is all done more easily by closing your eyes and sitting in a comfortable place, so I invite you to do so. Have gratitude for the trust the universe and the client have in you to bring you into this relationship. Take a deep breath and receive it. Breath in for a count of five, smile, hold it for five. Then breathe out for a count of five. Repeat a couple of rounds. Whisper "thank you." As Dr. Joe Dispenza says, "Gratitude is the ultimate state of receivership."
3. Envision your client, take a breath with them, and imagine them receiving your energy. Be gentle. There is no rush, and no coercion. Just imagine them entering your space and feeling safe, and smiling as you offer them some of the energy you are creating for them right now. Every meeting has a certain level of

energy transmitting from you to your client.

4. This is where you create some white space. White space is the area where you can envision and create with no projections, expectations, separations, judgments, or rejections. How's that? It really means you are in allowance of anything appearing. The more white space you can create, the more open you will be to receiving insights. This space has changed for me over time. I used to imagine a white wall or board, raise my eyebrows with curiosity, and allow any new ideas to pop up. It took some time before I gained the confidence that I wasn't "making it up." Even if I were making it up, it gave me a chance to inquire and create. Sometimes I imagine a field, a sky, an ocean. I raise my eyebrows with curiosity, no judgment, and ask what else I can receive for them. Sometimes I'll get a feeling. I will ask "what is it?" Don't look for answers, just stay curious. Answers send you down rabbit holes and cut you off from the flow.

5. Prepare to stay present. Tell yourself: "Whatever will be said in this meeting, I

am meant to hear it and ready and willing to hear it."
6. No assumptions, presumptions, or reactions. That's your stuff not your clients. No matter what happens or is said, stay curious and in allowance.
7. Be happy. This work is such a gift. It's a gift to the world, to your client, and to you. Smile, it's happening.

THE SESSION

There are many components of physical space and client experience which we will explore in other chapters that contribute to the magic. For now, I will jump right into the actual interaction between coach and client.

My clients usually like to give me the download of what has happened since we last met. Sometimes our most recent meeting was just a few days ago in which case they don't have as much to report, and this is when I will use my senses to dig into some areas which I noted require some attention. First, I usually let them set the agenda.

Bernard had been with me for many years and at times he jumped right into the storytelling and wanted to make sure we got everything covered so we discussed a meeting management strategy which I call three-in-three-out. We open the meeting by listing three topics, questions, or updates he wants to cover, and we close the meeting with three takeaways, to-dos or follow-ups. This completely changes the dynamic of the meeting and energizes it and makes it more fun as well as productive. Sometimes Bernard will show up and say he doesn't have that much to cover today and wasn't sure we even needed to meet and by the end of the session, we're both laughing at the depth we covered and what we unexpectedly cracked open.

So when a client shows up with a clear agenda, I tune my intuition to listen for what they are not saying. Yes, you heard me right. Of course I am listening with my ears, but I'm also listening with all my senses for any other information that is not verbal or literal. That's where the best questions come from.

Physically, what that means for me is sitting back a bit, taking it in, breathing into my belly while being completely present with my client. Being heard feels good. Silence is powerful. Do not underestimate it. You may even find you think of something and before you say it, they volunteer it or bring it up themselves.

Even though coaching education teaches us to ask questions and not give answers, coaches sometimes believe that they are adding value by analyzing the client and coming to conclusions.

You have to be aware of when you are doing this. I have done it, I still do it, and I catch myself more often than not. Sitting back and breathing into my belly grounds me back into the possibilities and not the conclusions. Every time you want to narrow in on an answer, you cut out other possible outcomes, including ones that even you can't imagine as possible. There are always, always more possibilities than you or your client are aware of. Keep your awareness open, keep asking questions, and keep your eyebrows away from the analytic narrowing or lowering into a frown.

The hardest thing to say sometimes is nothing. Just nod with understanding, acknowledge their feelings, and validate the normalcy of their experience, then give it space. You may even have to give it space until the next session. Is that too hard? I can't say this enough: *Trust* the process. Trust yourself and trust your client.

Now let's go back to the difference between thoughts and insights during the session. I believe that we are all intuitive and that with practice, it can easily integrate into our coaching to the point that we may not even notice we're receiving intuitive hits. It happens to me all the time. For a coach, intuition is not predicting the future for your client. It can come as knowing the right question to ask that leads to the breakthrough.

For example, Samir told me about some stress

at work and how frustrated he was about how his colleague is not listening to him and suddenly I think of Samir's mom. Yup, his mom. I have no idea why; I don't know Samir's mom. I get curious about why I might be thinking of his mom and wait for the moment to ask, "By the way, how's your mom?" Of course, Samir was a bit surprised but then he said, "It's so interesting you ask. I was having an argument with her this morning because she should be going to the doctor to have something checked out and she's just so stubborn." Hmm … isn't that interesting? Where's the stubborn colleague now? When you eventually go back to the stress at work, there may be a different energy around it, leaving space for other possibilities.

Trust yourself. I could've said to myself, "Mom? This is about work, don't go there." Or, "That's just too weird, if you ask about his mom he'll think you're being his therapist?" Instead, I just got curious, and was open to that "thought" being a contribution to our session. By the way, I could have been wrong, or the timing could have been off, in which case I just move on. Be in allowance at all times of your client, and of yourself. More times than not this degree of lightness and exploration will lead to something and when you acknowledge that you are open to receiving messages, and willing to experiment with them, you will receive more and more messages and get better at filtering through the most meaningful ones.

Let's move to a scenario in the session when your client shares something shocking or truly upsetting to you. I happen to coach a lot of clients who have not done a lot of inner work so as our relationship develops, they find themselves sharing things with me which they may not have ever shared with anyone else. Going back to step five in our prep, remember "whatever will be said in this meeting, I am meant to hear it and ready and willing to hear it." Nothing happens by accident. This is coming up for a reason and must be tied to something we are working on. It is my job to hold the space for them as they work through it. To some of you this may sound like therapy. Unlike some therapists, I am not looking to ease the pain or make them comfortable with what they have shared. I am looking to take them from one place to another, to shift paradigms, to help them change tracks. I am looking for the lock and the key to their greatness and I know that we have to go through the passage, not around it.

Again, I sit back, breathe into my belly and I just *be* space and allowance for them. The client will feel my compassion and the safe Space we have created and move through it. There is a strength in my presence that shows them I can handle anything they bring up and will stay with them. I bring up this example because I want you prepared for everything and I want you to see that you can *be* exactly who the client needs you to be at any moment, without having to *do* or *say* anything.

My experience tells me that the clients who are willing to put anything on the table, even if they are not sure why they are doing it, are the ones who will have the greatest professional breakthroughs as well. On the contrary, the ones who keep the agenda tight and narrow are managing their performance with me and looking for an A grade, which will also limit them at work as they rarely reveal who they truly are not only to others but to themselves, which eventually catches up on them.

My teacher Benjamin taught me that I can't take anyone's free will away. They have to be willing to choose growth and expansion. If they need to fall, they fall. I can't stop them, but I can be there when they do, with no judgment. Consistency in the coaching relationship is critical. Your client has to see that you are there for them no matter what.

Being all-in on the relationship also means I am not judging it, or them. It means I am in allowance for their process, and I keep a light heart throughout. This means I am present energetically, and when they go to their dark place, I always keep my hand on the light switch to bring them back.

This also means I don't judge myself. No "good coach, bad coach" stories. The session is never the time for that. If you want to keep improving your skills and get feedback on your performance as a coach, hire your own coach. Your client is not here to make you feel good.

POST-MEETING

Here you are, after a long day of clients, usually mid-week, and you have so much going on in your head from all the stories, the challenges, the lessons. What happens next?

Just like the session starts before the actual session, it also doesn't end. I found that when a client signed up to work with me for six months or a year at a time, they were always in my system. I would think about them, I would remember the important dates, meetings they prepped for, promotion announcement dates, bonus days, and of course birthdays. If it mattered to them, it mattered to me. I always want my client to feel loved and supported by me. There are times when my client can be going through an intense transition and we speak every day. Other times, they are in a flow, and we just meet when we meet which is usually every week or two. My client always knows, however, that I can ebb and flow with their needs.

It is quite common for a client to get a "how did the meeting go?" text from me shortly after the meeting took place. I always imagine what it would feel like if I got that text after something important took place for me. I give that kind of energy to my client and when they receive it, they are more likely to give it to someone else. We are creating an electric circuit of giving and they are plugging into it and plugging others into it. You will know your client is moving forward when they start influencing others and saying things like, "You'd be proud of me, one of my mentees was having a challenging week and I shared with them what you and I talked about last week."

When you go through the seven steps to prepare for your next meeting, and you get to the white space part where you are downloading on behalf of your client, you may realize you have been processing something for them since the last meeting, even on an unconscious level. One of the most powerful things you can start your next meeting with is: "I was thinking about you this week, and about how important trust is for you. How open are you to unpacking that a bit together?" The key phrase here is: "I was thinking about you." Try it out. You will feel the energy shift immediately. This is another aspect of holding

Space for them. It is warm, connected, and sincere and your client will feel it.

Stay in your body, stay present, keep an open mind and heart, and know with complete certainty that the connection between you and your client and the Space you hold for them will bring the magic. No doubt.

THE DEPARTMENT OF CORRECTIONS

I am sure you have noticed by now that we are living in two worlds at all times, like parallel processes. As a coach, you know it is all about the client. It is their agenda, you are there for them, in service to them, as a contributor to their success. At the same time, if you are still reading this book, you have accepted that your clients are your universal assignments and while it's not about you, it's also sometimes about you. How can that be? It is not your agenda; but your personal development work is part of your contribution to the relationship. If you offer your clients solutions and possibilities which you are not willing to embrace or engage in yourself, you will notice they fall flat. If you are not willing to hold yourself accountable, you will have a hard time holding your clients accountable. The more courageous you are to face your inner work, the more courageous your clients will be to embrace change.

There are two dimensions in play here. You are probably attracting people like you, and / or you are influencing their actions by your willingness to show up and play full out yourself. Or more likely both. It's a win-win.

One of the most important people in my life, Annie Fox, taught me some of the most valuable lessons. She was a healer, a spiritual mom, and a mentor to me. Sadly, she passed away many years ago, but her messages are still alive in my life, especially as a coach. When I left my career on Wall Street and became an executive coach she said, "Congratulations, we now have the same boss – The Department of Corrections."

For many of you with some spiritual background, you will know this aligns with many studies, including the one I get much of my inspiration from, Kabbalah. Ancient wisdom tells us the soul is on a journey through many lifetimes, each one, chosen by the soul, as a perfect environment full of opportunities to correct and cleanse past experiences through to the ultimate correction and completion of its process. What Annie meant was all of us who sign up to guide others on their paths to overcome and grow in the face of life's challenges are all working for the greater good to help these souls correct transgressions and regressions and return home.

So what does all this mean for us? It means that when you sign up to do this work, you too, get put through your paces. Like my client Rose said, "Oh great, another f-ing opportunity for person growth." Yes. Always another opportunity for personal growth. The Department of Corrections keeps you honest. The more invested you are in other people's success and fulfillment, the quicker your work will come at you.

WALK THE TALK

I had been in business for a few years already and had a lot of happy clients, a thriving business which hit seven figures in the third year, and I could not hire coaches quickly enough to meet the demand. I had so many happy clients, many of whom stayed in touch over the years. That is until this one November.

I had been sharing an office space with a friend for the first few years and I knew it was time to move on and sign a lease of my own, but I was nervous about the commitment. At the same time that I had started the company, Paul and I were also trying to have children, which had been challenging in my forties. Our daughter was born in April so I was hesitating to expand the company further and undertake a lease obligation, as a new mom. Everyone around me knew I had been talking about it for a while but going around in circles.

November seemed like a particularly sluggish month for my clients, especially Theresa, Joe, and Samantha. I felt like the sessions were déjá vus. I was used to big things happening for people, and pretty quickly, but I wasn't seeing much of it at this particular time. I was also tired, given my infant's sleep schedule and I didn't have my usual mojo.

Teresa had been referred to me by a close friend of mine, signed up with much fanfare. She had a big presence, a strong voice, and seemed self-assured. She was super excited about her fast-growing business and talking a big game about how in-demand she was. After three weeks, I noticed she was still trying to impress me and would not answer any question directly. I started challenging her a bit. She did not want to change the way she did things, and pushed back and justified her decisions, independent of anything we had worked on in session. I have to admit, I didn't know where this was going, and I had to work on my own view of my client as well. I was starting to question why she even hired me as her coach.

Joe was referred to me by one of my regular clients as a creative with lots of potential, ready to launch his own company. Or was he? Again, three or four weeks go by, Joe seems to have all the answers yet will not make a decision. I am wondering why he's even showing up to his sessions.

Samantha hired me to help her launch two ventures, neither of which she was willing to commit to completely as she valued her flexibility and was afraid she would lose it as a full-time entrepreneur. I walked home one night scratching my head. This was unusual, and exhausting. What was going on? Why wouldn't anyone make a decision this week? And then, the a-ha. Could it be that I'm vibrating at that frequency myself, seesawing between the security and comfort I have of a solid practice with low overhead, and taking the expansion risk? How can I expect others to be decisive and assertive when I was not willing to take the plunge? The next day, I went to see an available space in my building and signed a lease.

Something so interesting happened next. Teresa, Joe, and Samantha, almost simultaneously asked for a refund, as if this process was over for all of us at once. I can tell you as I write this book that this has never happened in more than twelve years, but it happened three times in one week. How is this possible? Well, as I have been saying, you will be held accountable. You will be asked to play full out when you ask others to play full out. You will be asked to be an inspiration and a guiding light. You have to be willing and able and committed if you want your clients to see results.

If you hesitate to do the work yourself, you will get instant feedback. This is a humbling craft. You will be shown, and you will be shown it fast, so get ready. It is as if I had attracted indecision through my indecision and when I shifted that, people who didn't want to shift exited the game. Perhaps they wanted a space to indulge in having options with no commitment and I was providing that by being in that space myself. They were in my movie to reflect back to me the responsibility I had to do the work as well. When I think of how I can inspire others through my actions, I am always motivated into action. Inspiring and guiding others to become aware of and to achieve their greatness is my mission.

In an interview with Marie Forleo, Dr. Joe Dispenza shared a secret to his leadership and the success of his business which has made and continues to make a tremendous contribution to the world through popular meditation events where thousands of people meditate together, dance, and learn together. I have been to several of his events and have witnessed spontaneous, miraculous healings. I am inspired by Dr. Joe and others who are not only able to create new ways to make major contributions to the lives of others but also know how to grow successful, large, impactful businesses.

When asked how he does what he does and how he has built a team who is aligned with him and extremely effective at helping him grow his business, he refers to research that was done to understand motivation. He explains the sequence of five types of motivation.

Mission is the highest form of motivation. People who are mission motivated have a purpose, a vision that is greater than them. That is the reason they get up in the morning. Being connected to a mission is the highest level of motivation. The next level of motivation is personal conviction motivation. These are people who say they're going to do something, and they do it because they are convicted. They have a high level of motivation based on their personal conviction but it's not as high as mission motivation. People who have mission motivation, naturally have personal conviction motivation.

The next form of motivation is ethics or morality motivation. People who are driven by ethics motivation function in polarity: good and bad, right and wrong. People who truly have a mission are naturally driven by personal conviction and they have ethics and morality. The next level is self-aggrandizement motivation – "hey look at how great I am." By the way, the lowest form of motivation is money but if you follow the sequence from the mission down, and you follow the money-making tips I share with you in a later chapter, you will do what you love and make lots of money doing it. Start from the mission, and you will have it all.

There will be times when you will have so much mojo as a coach that it will feel like everything you touch turns to gold. I had many years like that and they're awesome. There will also be times when you feel a bit more tired, and it feels like stories are repeating themselves and you wish more were happening for your clients. In those times, take yourself back to why you are doing this. If you are motivated by money, you won't last. If you are motivated by being a teacher and showing people the right ways versus the wrong ways of doing things, you won't last. You will only create a sustainable future if you are always clear about your mission and aligned with it. Most importantly, if you do deviate or get distracted, then you know how to bring yourself back.

When things slow down as they sometimes do, ask yourself: "What can I *be* or *do* differently to be an invitation and an inspiration for clients who want to play full out and win?" You won't always hear an answer or have an answer but just by asking the question, you will show up to be the change, and that will get the wheels turning again.

JUMP RIGHT IN

Jeff was lacking energy and motivation, and just came into his sessions each week a bit discouraged that things weren't changing at work even though his bosses said they intended to promote him. Each week he started the session with more stories and examples of how wrong everyone was at work for not putting him in charge and how he had made a mistake joining this company in the first place. I would try various techniques and approaches to help him see things differently, but he was stuck. I recognized a pattern. He was presenting as the victim to everybody else's actions and decisions, but I picked up on a deep disappointment he had with himself.

> Jeff: "My boss, who was my peer until this recent promotion, is undermining me. I feel like he's trying to get me fired."
>
> Me: "Tell me more."
>
> Jeff: "Every time I present a new idea, he takes credit for it then sends me on a wild goose chase for a project that doesn't even matter. He doesn't respect me."

Me: "How else is he not showing you respect?"

Jeff: "He works directly with my team without even telling me."

Me: "How does this make you feel about this job?"

Jeff: "I always end up in the same situation, I never should've gone into finance. I'm just not cut out for this, plus, I don't know how to define my job at the moment. I've done a terrible job creating a brand for myself. I don't even like working here. I should look for another job, but I don't want people to think I failed again."

That was a lot. In the end, it had nothing to do with his boss but rather how he was judging his career decisions, and his ability to carve a valuable niche for himself.

I shifted the focus to what he was doing to make himself happy rather than how other people were making him unhappy. As happens frequently with overworked clients, the first thing he told me was how he used to work out all the time but that it just got away from him and he complained about how he hadn't gone to the gym in months, and as a result he was probably having a couple of drinks too many to reduce his stress, which of course was affecting his sleep and his relationships because he just needed to be alone to unwind after a long day. I asked what it would take to break the cycle and got a couple of lukewarm "I can try to go to the gym this week." The likelihood of that was pretty slim but I went with it. Of course, the next week, not only did he not break the cycle, he then doubled-down on how much of a disappointment he was to not even be able to do that. When you have a client who's feeling defeated, you can be the most genius coach but until you help them get their mojo back, nothing will happen.

Jeff was having a hard time getting himself to the gym. I thought making it part of his commitment between sessions would work, but it didn't. There was something else going on. He knew going to the gym would give him more energy, but he needed a fire-starter. I had to do something unique here. "Jeff, what if I also commit to going to the gym at 6:00 a.m. tomorrow and we can text each other when we walk in the door at the gym? You don't even have to work out. You can just text me and say you're there."

Well, what do you know? We broke the cycle. Notice I did not say, "You have to be there forty-five minutes, and text me at the end of your workout to let me know you ran on the treadmill and lifted weights." I just said I care enough to do this with you and all you have to do is show up. I also didn't have to do it many more times. Just enough for him to get his mojo back and create a new habit for himself. Once he started feeling good about himself for working out again, he started eating better, drinking less, and he was in a better mood each time I saw him. Things lightened up at work too and at the end of that year, he even got the promotion.

ENDLESS POSSIBILITIES IN CO-CREATION

"Every definition, conclusion, and limitation you are willing to give up opens up a totally different possibility."

— DAIN HEER

THE PIPE

Imagine you and your body are like a big, long white PVC pipe. Insights come in from the top, and flow through you, to your client. The wider and cleaner the inside of your pipe, the brighter and more plentiful the insights, guidance, and brilliant questions which will flow through. Your job is to keep the pipe wide and clean with the top and bottom open.

Let's work through this together. Imagine the

input is low and you are not seeking your sources of inspiration, what happens to the top of your pipe? It narrows and even closes since there's no flow inward. You may not even believe that we have access to greater consciousness, where endless possibilities exist. I may be stretching your mind a bit but if this is not true to you at all, you probably would've stopped reading a few chapters ago.

There are great coaches who do not tap into spiritual wisdom or higher consciousness to inspire and support their coaching, at least not that they know of. The even greater ones do not limit themselves to this physical right or wrong, good or bad, win or lose reality. You don't have to be a spiritual coach or even speak a spiritual language. I rarely do that overtly. I do, however, keep going back to my sources of inspiration to stay in the flow and have access to an unlimited universe of possibilities, not just the ones I can think of in my head or from my experience. I say this not from faith but from experience. When you start noticing you are not operating alone, you will open the channels for greater receiving. What you will make available to your clients will go way beyond what you ever thought was possible.

Many great coaches I know have awareness of energy beyond the physical. However, they also may just be tapping into it through somebody else or something else. Take Brené Brown for example. She's a hard-core emotions researcher, specializing in vulnerability and shame. She does not at all come across woo-woo. Listening to her go one by one through the different emotions in *Atlas of the Heart* is somewhat of an intellectual exercise. However, she crossed out the word "breakdown" and replaced it with "spiritual awakening" because she realized that what seems like a moment of coming apart actually provided the basis for growth on a higher level of awareness.

She has always gone to church regularly and believes there are higher powers at play. The top of her pipe is open. She taps into greater sources which center and inspire her so she can keep the top of her pipe open and inspire others.

While we're on Brené Brown, she also keeps the inner walls of her pipe clean by keeping her ego in check. She has confidence in the magnitude of her ability to impact others and she is also aware that losing her humility will tighten the pipe and dirty the inner walls to the point that she will not be able to let the inspiration flow through. She takes deep topics like shame and vulnerability and makes them digestible through her self-deprecating humor. She is funny. She models responsibility and accountability to her audience by doing the work herself and speaking openly about it. It also helps that she can back it up with hard core data as well. She's an inspiration! Watching her Netflix special lecture was like watching an hour of stand-up but better, because you also walk away educated. Vulnerability keeps the pipe clean so the magic she communicates to her listeners does not get stuck in the webs of her ego on the way through.

Now let's say you just went and consumed knowledge, insights, lessons, wisdom, teaching from all around the world, and did not share all that to contribute to others. Say you just kept it all for yourself because you just like to learn and feel smart. The bottom of your pipe would close. What do you think will happen next? "More for me, more for me, more for me, look how smart I am, look how much I know, all for me." Can you imagine the flow getting sluggish, and lethargic, and full? It might even explode. The key is to share, share, share. The more you share, the more you receive. The more you receive, the more you can share. Keep the top and bottom of your pipe open and the inner walls clear.

The pipe taps you into a real-time knowing that never runs out. When you need more, you sit back, breathe, raise your eyebrows and ask for some guidance. My client Denise was telling me how she felt stuck in a client meeting, not knowing which direction to go next, and she just sat back in her chair and took a breath. The next idea then came to her, and she was able to redirect the discussion. Just that instinctual move to sit back and lower her space walls created the space to get back into flow again. She said, "When I'm engaged and warm, I'm all those things you remind me to be." Creating space just brings out more of Denise. It is the not knowing that gives you access to the greater knowing. Be the space. Stay in flow. You are purely a facilitator.

THE ANSWERS

The alternative to the pipe is a more finite existence. It's filling your cup and only sharing from that cup. Let's say I base my coaching on my acquired skills, knowledge, and experience which I acquired through my degrees in finance, and my career on Wall Street. There's a lot of good stuff there but I can tell you after thirteen years, it gets a bit stale and I would keep repeating myself. I would present myself as the answers and not the questions. I would act like an expert but in reality, as wide as the breadth of my career was in finance, I saw only the tiniest sliver of the pie. No way could I tell you all the different ways the client's scenario can play out.

KNOWLEDGE

The knowledge I have access to is limited. Knowledge is full of conclusions and judgments. In fact, throughout our careers we receive positive reinforcement for our judgment. When presented with a situation, the quicker we can draw a conclusion, the more valuable we are. The sooner we can eliminate all the possibilities, the smarter we appear. Sure, that's one answer, but is that all? By choosing that one possibility, are we limiting the others?

In *Breaking the Habit of Being Yourself*, Dr. Joe Dispenza wrote about how something is not real until it is observed and that once it becomes observed, it becomes real. This confused me too when I first read it. I then remembered my teacher Sara giving me a tool when I get triggered. I say to myself, "Don't make it significant," and just like that the oppressive energy doesn't feel so heavy anymore. Remember the State, Story, Strategy model? Saying to myself "Don't make it significant" can change my state and I have access to a different point of view. Making something significant makes it more real. There is certainly a lot in life to take seriously but you know that you sometimes make things more significant than they need to be, then you adapt your behaviors to that interpretation, which you then get a reaction to from others and now it's snowballing. Your point of view just created your reality. What would have happened if you just had not made it significant? Would it have become real? Or did it become real because you perceived it as real. Don't *figure* it out. *Try* it out. Don't make it significant.

KNOWING

Unlike knowledge, the knowing I have access to is limitless. What are the infinite possibilities? What would it take for this situation to create different results? I don't look to answer these questions, but just asking them, makes me zoom out and create space for a different reality to unfold. I switch from a linear world to a non-linear world away from the time and space I expect things to play out in. A powerful and simple homework I give to my over-thinking, problem-solving clients is to say "I don't know" more. It is quite unnatural. Can you raise your eyebrows with curiosity and wonder and say, "I don't know"? What happens to your body and your energy? Do your shoulders go up or down? Do you lean forward or backward? Do you look up and around? Does it feel like you are in for a little surprise? Have fun with it. Let's see what happens.

The brain has knowledge; the gut knows. "I don't know" allows your brain to let go a bit so you can sense your inner knowing. Once you have released the "figuring it out" energy that is constricting, you can then ask very powerful questions. What *do* you know? What do you pretend not to know that if you did know would change everything?

Trust yourself and trust the process. Keep the pipe open and let it flow.

THE COACH'S EGO

In his documentary *I'm Not Your Guru*, Tony Robbins talks about how the coach is not the guru. He says the client has all the answers. Your client is not broken; they don't need you to fix them. They have patterns that give momentum and growth, and they have other patterns that get in their way. In fact, you don't even need to know where those patterns come from or why they exist. You do have the senses to recognize them and teach your clients to recognize them as well, so they can help themselves when you are not around. The coaching model is an action-oriented empowering model. I like to be transparent with my client about what I see and feel so that they can walk away with their pattern recognition skills.

My client Ellen was self-aware and self-critical. It was part of her defense mechanism, as if being her own judge and jury would protect her from judgment. Ironically, what it did do is create an energy around her that would make her more susceptible than protected. I had been working with her on and off for years and had recognized a pattern that kept reemerging. Not knowing why, there were many situations where she just didn't feel "liked." She was in a leadership role in finance and was accomplished, and super driven. She was not someone you would expect to be measuring "likeability" but that was her thing.

When she felt like someone just didn't like her, she would get defensive and even paranoid about her job. It was hard to ration with her so I would not. What I did notice is the pattern of defensive behavior, which would then lead others to exclude her or act suspiciously around her. This defensiveness would lead her to write the long emails, and drift away from her strengths for building relationships and growing businesses. Any time I saw her preparing to give somebody a piece of her mind, I recognized the defensiveness and that was my cue to go upstream and look for where she felt rejected and unliked.

As a coach, it's tempting to get into a back and forth of right and wrong, good and bad but it does not matter. This was true for her. It may not have been the truth, but it's true for her. If I am trying to prove to her how untrue her belief is, then it's my ego against hers, even though her ego is pretending to play small, her defensiveness is ego. It's protective and it won't let anyone close to her real being. So when I recognized the pattern, I coached upstream of it. "I can see how something triggered you into feeling rejected or unliked. I'm not surprised, given the importance of this partnership to you. What happened?" This would inevitably lead to her telling a story of where the personal connections were at work and where they did not include her.

When you go back to the core emotion, and untangle it there, you can repattern the response. By doing this enough times, and she can lean into doing it herself, and she can learn a different reaction which will become natural over time.

We all have our dark place; it is just a matter of how often we go there and how long we stay. Decreasing the duration and frequency by any amount can have dramatic results.

As you can see, your role does not change. You are allowing the possibilities to flow through you with questions, as opposed to having answers come from you to solve problems.

I'M EXHAUSTED

At the risk of oversimplifying, your presence as a coach is either loving or in judgment. There isn't much in between. Lovingness and care come from the heart; judgment comes from the mind, which is also where the ego plays tricks on you. The ego expresses itself in five ways: anger, pride, control, judgment, and hatred. The ego gives you physiological feedback. It's a gift. If you embrace this awareness, you will become an amazing coach.

The ego will also have different behaviors at different stages of your coaching career. Early in my coaching career I was amazed at how I could coach all day every day and not get tired. I would meet my first client at 8:00 a.m., see a few more before lunchtime, close a new lead over a one-hour lunch, rush back to the office to see clients all afternoon, then bounce out at the end of the day with more energy than I had at 8:00 a.m.

I was in a good flow, and I was quite confident that my system was working. Confidence does not have to be ego. When you are mission motivated, it's easier to be confident because you know what you are doing is helping others. That wasn't the sign of my ego. The clue was exhaustion one day. I dragged out of the office, slowly putting one foot in front of the other walking home, feeling somewhat defeated and definitely tired. What happened? I couldn't understand.

I didn't have an unusually busy day, I had slept well the night before, I had even walked to work on that beautiful spring day and had a healthy lunch. What could it be? Then I remembered this one session I had with Jon who was complaining that he had already had eight sessions out of the ten he had paid for, and he still didn't have a new job in sight. I kept trying to do some inner work with him so that he could come across with more energy and sincerity and he just wouldn't go there. He wanted the tactical work – LinkedIn, networking, interview skills.

Jon and I had worked together in the past and knew a lot of the same people so I really wanted him to have a good experience. I was trying to accommodate and convince him of a different way when he was just not bought in. I was also doing it in a way which was not as direct as I would have been with other clients because I didn't want him to feel pushed. There was resistance in our relationship on both sides. I tried to control him by giving him homework he wasn't agreeing to, especially if soft skills were involved. He tried to control me by measuring results from session to session, and we were both trying to control results.

Furthermore, I took the feedback personally when he was disappointed with the results, and I judged him and myself in the process. Exhaustion is a sign that your ego is in play. When you are in flow, and staying true to your mission to hold Space and honor the experiences people require for their growth, you won't get attached to the results. Miraculously, they will get better results because neither of you is suffocating the process. What he was saying was not my truth, but it was true to him and it didn't have to be about me. It could have been his frustration with himself. If my ego didn't jump in the game, I would have had compassion for him and worked through the disappointment with him without making it personal. It could have been a breakthrough for him. The minute I made it about me and my performance, I disconnected.

BURNOUT

Managing your ego is also how you avoid burnout. Nothing will burn you out quicker than your ego. There could be a sneaky little voice in your head that says, "Oh, if I coach that person, it will make me look good." Watch out for the WIIFM. The WIIFM is a coaching tool that helps you position things to the benefit of your prospect or client who are viewing things through the lens of "What's In It For Me." When the coach is looking for their WIIFM, it does not work out so well. I am always amazed at how quickly the feedback comes.

I could get a call that the head of HR of a trillion-dollar company wants me to coach their CEO. I immediately tune-in to my senses and ask myself to feel the person and "what's going on for them and how can I help?" just as if it was my first client so many years ago. If I get impressed or nervous or excited about what it means for me, I'm likely to not win the opportunity.

Just like my client Alex asked, "I had this amazing lead, it would have been a high-profile client, really good for my company, but I didn't get the business, I don't understand why." WIIFM.

Each client is a soul-level assignment, don't get distracted by labels and wardrobe. Looking for the WIIFM will not only push business away, it will leave you dissatisfied and confused as to why you are feeling so tired and defeated. How did you make this about you?

When I get distracted from my why I am in this work, then my ego shows me WIIFM to coach someone and somehow things don't work out. The contract doesn't get signed, the sessions are hard to schedule, the deal falls through. Of course, I benefit from having clients, and my business benefits, etcetera, but if I keep the mission in the forefront, and remain in service to them, then I will always be taken care of.

The ego will wear me down. Any time spent frustrated, judging myself or my clients, controlling the outcome, wanting to be seen a certain way will drain me and eventually burn me out. Listen, we are human, these things will happen, you just have to recognize your patterns and interrupt them before they gain momentum. Dr. Joe Dispenza explains that the stronger the emotional reaction you have to some experience in your life, the more attention your brain will pay to that emotion, and it will create a snapshot of that experience which is called a memory.

If you replay that memory over and over for days, it turns into a mood. "Why are you in the mood?" Because of what happened five days ago which you keep replaying as if it is still happening. When that mood lasts for weeks and weeks, it turns into a temperament. "Why is he so bitter? Oh, because of that thing that happened months ago." At this rate, the temperament becomes a personality trait which is harder and harder to change.

The hardest part about change is not making the same choices you made the day before and not recreating the same emotions from thoughts alone. This is why it is so important to recognize your patterns and interrupt them. Otherwise, your ego is running the show and showing you all the reasons why you need to be guarded and distant and calculating and mistrusting. How is this serving you?

The more you care about your own state, the less likely this is to happen to you and your business. Maybe you need a long weekend, a vacation, a fun night out with your friends. Maybe your receiving tank is empty and requires a refill. There is nothing wrong with that. When you feel your ego, and I promise you will feel it if you pay attention, pause, interrupt the pattern, and find your way back home to your mission. Take care of yourself so others will learn to take care of themselves too. You are an inspiration. Choose for yourself and inspire others.

IT'S A 3D JOURNEY

Another reason I currently engage in a minimum of six-month engagements is to give time and space for the magic to unfold and not judge progress one session at a time. It's a journey. There are many phases to the development process.

Discovery: First you establish the trust and safety in the relationship which is a discovery period for the coach and the client. It happens in the first few weeks.

Data: It takes about three to six weeks as well to collect the data, which is the information you require to make a development plan from. For executive coaching clients, this comes from assessments, stakeholder interviews, a meeting with the manager, and your assessment from the first few sessions.

Development: The growth and development starts happening from the first meeting. It is enhanced, however, by the collection of data and creation of the development plan. In a six-month engagement, months three to six see the greatest changes. Extending the coaching another six months after that ensures the sustainability of those changes for longer-term impact.

I lay this out here, in this manner, in this section so you and your client move away from session-to-session thinking. Each session has its own place. Some sessions will feel tactical, solving a live problem, preparing for an important presentation, scripting an opportunity to have a constructive confrontation. Other sessions will give you Space to explore greater possibilities more strategically or directionally. Your ego will want to measure. Measure progress, measure results. What did Kenny Rogers say in *The Gambler*? "Don't count your money when you're sitting at the table." Stay in flow. Keep doing everything we are talking about and you will have so much success you'll never have to count. I sometimes do three-hour deep-dive sessions with my clients when I feel we need to get somewhere that may not be available in a one-hour session. I learned this from my coach Nate Cantor. He knew how to break my ego. When I was leaving Wall Street thinking about my next move, he took me on as a client and would insist that all our sessions be three hours long. Just the thought of sitting there talking for three hours seemed like too much, but I trusted him. After a few of these sessions I realized he was onto something.

The first hour I would put on my best behavior – ambitious high-performer. I wanted to impress Nate. He had been a successful executive as COO of MCI WorldCom and was taking me under his wing. I wanted to be a "good" client. By the second hour, I was starting to tire and soften, in a better state to receive. By the third hour, I had lost it. My shoulders had dropped, I was totally open, and vulnerable. There were some tears, and real progress was made. Nate had cracked me. Sadly, within six months of our relationship, Nate was suddenly diagnosed with lung cancer and passed away. He was a great man and brilliant mentor. I am honored to have learned from him and become a coach by inspiration. I still think about him and wonder what Nate would have said now.

I learned from him to not have a fixed plan for any session. Our judgment and conclusion of the session can create new limitations for our client. Keep the Space open and free flowing which means keeping your junk out of it. Go into every session knowing there are infinite possibilities available for your client and just be the guide to the exploration.

One session does not stand on its own. It's part of a greater journey. If you set expectations and measurements, then you block the flow. You also start evaluating better or worse sessions which ultimately means evaluating your performance. This is a buzz kill.

I urge you to maintain a regular rhythm with your client so you do have time and space for deeper dives and breakthroughs. I have found that if we do not meet often, then we stay in a tactical, problem-solving space rather than a deep development, paradigm shifting space.

My client George was always too busy, always complaining about his schedule and how everything was an emergency he had to attend to. He would come to our sessions with a list of situations that needed to be addressed urgently, which we did, but it was hard to get past the fire fighting to do some of the deeper development work. You want to have some calm space to say, "I was thinking about something you said a couple of weeks ago and wonder if you are open to unpacking it a bit today?" Then you can go somewhere that can provide a more foundational shift.

In George's case, I had to get him away from his desk and all the interruptions. We went out for a shot of tequila and dinner and he opened up some personal challenges he had overcome which were influencing him at work. We talked about how far he's come and what he envisions his future to look like and what he is doing to contribute to or distract from his goals. It was nice to have a chance to zoom out. It was a three-hour session and it worked. Thank you, Nate.

It is important to recognize how your client shows up in indifferent environments. Try to mix it up. You may find a phone session can reveal something a video or in-person session does not. Lunch or dinner might open them up to discuss some personal aspirations which are contributing to their professional goals. Trust your gut to know what is right and when for each client. Some clients can get right into it in their glass office while people are walking by. Others might need to be out of their environment.

Henry was an interesting client. He was very invested in his image of being a very successful hedge fund manager. He would not show me any weaknesses. I picked up that confronting him directly could put his ego on the defensive so I took the first few sessions to build trust. One day, he emailed and said he was stuck in the office and could not come to me. We jumped on the phone instead. This must have felt safe to him in that moment because he immediately revealed an insecurity and even asked for my help. I took this window of opportunity to candidly share an observation I had made from our meetings which may also be showing up in other relationships and it turned into a breakthrough. We revealed that he considered keeping personal distance to be "professional." We explored how he could maintain a professional space while offering more vulnerability to allow people to connect with him. My hunch on the phone format for this conversation was spot on.

JUDGING YOUR CLIENT

Francisco was a new coach. He had come out of the technology industry as a manager and was excited about coaching. He had heard about me and hired me right away to learn how to replace the significant income he had just walked away from. One particularly meaningful session, he was airing frustration about how he knew this guy Zain who went to a new company and they had been talking about Francisco doing a program there but Zain was slow in getting it approved. Francisco was so annoyed with him. It was a West Coast engagement, and he wanted to plan his family's summer vacation around it and needed an answer. My spidey senses were up. He was judging his client, and that never works. I gave him homework. I asked him to send me an email with a list of ways he made the engagement with Zain all about him. Ego alert. A couple of hours later, this is the email I got from him.

"The 9 Ways I made Zain about me.

1. *Getting a West Coast client ensures some West Coast credibility in case my family wants to move back.*
2. *TechCo is an awesome client to reference to people within technology – "you must be a great coach if you work with TechCo."*
3. *I've told people that TechCo is about to become a client but they're not officially – Integrity.*
4. *Securing TechCo puts me over 200K for the year and few coaches have had that type of success in their 1st year.*
5. *I flew all the way out there, left my family, and Zain disrespected my time.*
6. *Getting Zain as a client gives me a chance to network with bigger books of business at TechCo.*
7. *Flying back and forth to LA gets my United Airlines FF miles status and miles back up – i.e., free vacation travel.*
8. *If I can turn engineering professionals (i.e., Zain's direct reports) into marketers, I can turn anyone into a marketer – a.k.a. – I just made myself the hero.*
9. *Even my non-tech friends know TechCo – "Hey, this coaching thing is going to work."*

Thanks for a great session. It was emotionally draining and awesome.
On my drive home, I got a text from Zain,
"Paperwork has been approved and sent over to get a PO.
Enjoy your Thanksgiving."

His personal development work unblocked the approval process. Brilliant. This is how the system works. You will see for yourself.

ACKNOWLEDGE YOURSELF

If you're looking for feedback, get your own coach – don't look for your client to acknowledge you. The coaches who hired me as their coach early in their journeys accelerated their growth to top revenues and sharp skills quickly. It was fun work too. They would come in each week and go through their client scenarios, and it was like doing live case studies. They would try something new with a client, come back and report how it went, we would refine the skills and off they went. They were the inspiration for this book because I realized how much I had to share and how much I loved to share what made me a successful coach.

Resist the temptation to look for compliments from your client. Even when they say I am amazing, I smile and give them a hug. Of course I want to sit down and have them tell me 101 ways I'm an amazing coach but if I do, I run the risk of a) aiming to please and get the same reaction in our next meeting which will kill my flow, b) starting to judge myself against a new standard we just set, and c) looking to receive energy from my clients and when they don't give it because that's not their job, I could feel deflated and tired. It's an ego trap. Stay away.

There may be times when you question how much contribution you are making. It happens. Are you motivated by your mission? Are you doing your personal development work? Are you keeping your ego out of it? Are you showing up with an open heart and mind? Are you being true to you? Are you keeping your energy tank full? If yes, Acknowledge yourself. This is the best job in the world and you are doing great.

MONEY IS ENERGY

"If you want to be rich, simply serve more people."

— ROBERT KIYOSAKI

Have you met my friend Money?

I have heard so many stories and myths and limiting beliefs about money over the years. There was a time when I was regularly doing a two-hour money session which was a deep dive into my client's relationship with money. I noticed that most people saw money as something separate from them, usually slightly out of reach, at least to the degree they wanted.

Our relationship with money runs deep. Do you remember your first interaction with money? Was it an allowance from your parents? Was it from your first job? Was it a birthday gift your grandparents gave you? Do you remember opening your first bank account or having your first ATM card and magically pulling $20 out of the wall?

My earliest memories of money were that there just wasn't enough of it. There was a brief time when my dad was establishing his business that we were finally able to buy a house in Montreal, but my parents divorced that same year and then the financial gap between what my mom needed to raise my brother and me and what she had available to do so was obviously big. I remember Thursday being payday for her and she would go straight to the grocery store with her earnings and spend almost all of it feeding us. We were well aware of how far each day was from the next paycheck. I was thirteen and too young to work but when I turned fourteen and the owner of a sandwich shop in the food court asked me how old I was, I said sixteen so I could get the job.

"Would you like fries with that?"

Something clicked inside me with that job. I realized money wasn't a problem or something to fight over. Money was available and it was my friend. With money I could go places, have fun and freedom, I could buy clothes and shoes. Life was fun with money. Money was empowering. I also realized I loved to work and the more I worked, the more money I made, the more independent I became. Money gave me a sense of control. Which teenager doesn't want control?

Do you remember money becoming your friend? Or do you remember money always being just out of reach? Do you remember your parents fighting over money and you thinking money causes problems between people? Or do you remember your grandparents giving you money with a big smile and the excitement that you could buy whatever you wanted? What do you remember?

Here's a little exercise for you. Spend a few minutes writing these out. It can be telling.

- What do you *love* about money?
- What do you *hate* about money?

It's easy to say we all love money, but we often have a subconscious love-hate relationship with money that can keep the endless flow of it distant from us. There is no reason for money NOT to come to you with ease, unless you have a reason for blocking it. You see, money is universal energy. And energy always wants to contribute to your life.

If you are reading this book, it's because you want the world to be a better place and you want to contribute to making it so. Can you change the world more with money or without money? With!

So then if your mission is to contribute to the lives of others, then the universe wants to give you money to do so.

If you do discover that there is some reason you do hate money, as hard as that is to admit, then get curious and ask yourself who you bought that from, and does it belong to you? If not, thank it for trying to protect you, and release it and send it home. Anytime you feel a limitation or a blockage around money, get curious, ask where it came from, thank it, and send it back.

MONEY IS JUST AN EXCHANGE OF ENERGY

Have you ever noticed that you sometimes receive more from something you pay a lot for? Do you value an expensive pair of shoes more than the flip-flops you picked up at the pharmacy? Sometimes. Do you take advice from a consultant you paid a lot of money to but not from a friend over dinner who's just as qualified? Sometimes.

When your client pays you for a service, like coaching, it is their way of returning energy to you for what they are receiving. When this exchange is in balance, the energy flows and everyone benefits from the relationship. When one side of the relationship tips the balance off, the energy stops flowing. For example, if you have a client who begged for a discount (which was your first no-no), then calls, texts, and emails you every day and won't leave at the end of the session, then you will eventually feel like the energy exchange is off. The other way, not paying enough, will have you feeling like you have so much to give to your client, and they are just not engaged.

Both sides have to be fully committed for the relationship to drive results for your client. Pricing your services right, and your client paying for them as per your payment standards, is one way to start the relationship off in balance.

YOUR SELF-WORTH IS NONE OF THEIR BUSINESS

I have coached a lot of coaches over the years, and almost all of them, including myself, have a price at which we question whether we are that valuable. This is completely normal. Coaching is personal, and I am sure you have found that it does not feel that different from what you have been doing your whole life, wanting to support others through challenges, but you never thought you could make money doing it.

When it comes time to charge for something you have always done for free, these questions will come up. Remember, you're a great coach because you would do it for free. If you do it for free, your contributions will be limited.

There are two reasons for this.

- You need to create a sustainable future for yourself and your business so you can be of service to many people. If you can't afford to stay in the business forever, you will not be of much use to anyone.
- Your client needs to pay for it so they can receive from you. In fact, they need to pay an amount that is meaningful enough to them to take it seriously. Remember my examples of the first few clients I wanted to gift coaching to, and they were not engaged until they started paying for it?

So back to self-worth. What you charge for coaching has nothing to do with what you believe your time is worth, or what you are worth. Money is not proof of your worth. You are not pricing your worth. You are pricing the value you are contributing to their lives. Keep them separate. This is not a feedback mechanism for you to feel valuable or accomplished. It is normal to feel good about your work, it's great work, just don't use it to compensate for a lack of something else. Almost all coaches have had to break through this at some point.

Any time you find the little voice in your head asking, "Are you going to charge that much for your sessions?" reply with a confident, "Absolutely!" I will show you how and why. By the way, I've seen coaches hesitate to charge $100 per session or $2,000 per session just the same. We all have a price at which we question if we are worth that. Your coaching fees have nothing to do with your self-worth. The sooner you dissociate the two, the quicker your business will grow and the more people you will be of service to.

FIRST ONE'S ON ME

Remember how I started my business by giving away the first session. I still do. Once again, I will ask you to live in two worlds. Have a generous spirit of contribution, while at the same time know the price has to create a sustainable future and a fair energy exchange.

Here's how this looks. You go out to dinner with some friends, you share with a new friend that you're a coach. They share some challenges they could use some help with. You tell them you'd love to brainstorm with them about it and set up a follow-up conversation over coffee. When you go to meet them, you are ready to enter into a client-coach relationship with them by the end of the hour. This might feel like sales to you, and it is. There is nothing wrong with that. You have solutions for them, which they would love to pay for and receive. You have a system by which they can receive that from you so let's do this.

CHEMISTRY MEETING

Allow me to get a little technical here because I want you to walk away with the exact how-tos as well as the inspiration.

You get to the coffee place twenty minutes early, you ground yourself and do the pre-meeting prep we laid out in Chapter 6. You walk into the meeting with a warm smile, open heart and curious mind. You are grateful that you are being given this opportunity and get excited to be a part of the future for this new client. You got this.

Even if you're at a Starbucks, remember it's your Space. That might mean you pick the seat and get the coffee order. Owning the Space also means managing the time. Let's say you both agree you have an hour. It is your job to manage that hour in three parts.

The Download

You ask them to tell you what's going on and you can take notes and listen with mostly non-verbal cues for twenty minutes. You can ask some quick clarifying questions like "why did you leave that job?" but you're mostly listening. You can add some brief connection comments like "I also went to Michigan. Class of '06." Then you urge them to keep going. This is mostly them telling you their story. In twenty minutes, it's time to move into the next phase. If you do not, you will probably not have time to close it, and they will walk away unsatisfied. This twenty-minute mark is critical to the close.

Coaching Teaser

You thank them for sharing all that with you. If they are still going at a 100 miles per hour, you just interrupt with, "Mind if I jump in here? You've given me a lot to work with and we will have time for more. Thank you." Now you start coaching. Here's the key for this portion. You want to feed back to them, something you picked up and interpreted which they did *not* tell you. Huh? Here's an example. "I am picking up from your story, that work has always played such a significant role in your life, and much of your identity has been wrapped around your professional success, usually through greater salaries and promotions working for others." Pause and give them a chance to acknowledge or comment. "With that, it sounds to me that you are ready to integrate that into a greater life, perhaps even as an entrepreneur, or a creator. How do you feel when you hear these words?"

There are a million possibilities here, you are just coaching. You are acknowledging having received what they shared with you, and giving them a taste of what it feels like to be asked intuitive, insightful questions. You are also giving them a teaser of that awesome feeling of being understood and guided to greater possibilities. Within minutes, they will feel like this could work for them and you care enough to be there with them while it unfolds.

The Close

Your prospect is probably getting pretty excited at this forty-minute mark and is wondering how much this is going to cost. They will probably ask, "How does it work?" Which is their way of asking how much but I don't tell them how much until the end. When they ask how it works, I go into logistics with a presumptive close. "Well, as soon as we're done, you'll get an email from my assistant with engagement details to sign and pay for, and she will get you scheduled for your first session. I suggest you find a similar time which may work for you each week, so you spend less time on the back and forth. Once all that is taken care of, we will send you a link to an assessment, which you will love. It is the most powerful assessment on the market. You will be amazed how deep we will get in a short amount of time. My goal is for you to start feeling the shifts and seeing results within three to four weeks. The assessment helps us do that. How does this all sound for you?"

At this point, if they are paying themselves versus their company paying for them, they will probably hone in more on how much it will cost. I continue, "We will meet almost every week, in-person, in my office (or wherever you choose), and if we can't make it in person, we will meet by video or phone. I want you to feel supported between sessions as well so you can text me anytime and if we need to jump on a call quickly because something came up, you will have my number. You might need to take a walk around the block and call me instead of hitting send on a heated email. It's all good."

If it's a corporate engagement and the company is paying, I will close here with "How does this all sound to you?" and get the first session scheduled. If it is a company owner, or an entrepreneur paying for themselves, I'll give them the cost, and let them know the terms, which are usually all up-front and we move on. Got it? Are you ready?

The thing about the payment is that you want to deal with it once, and be done. This is why I always ask for payment up front if the individual is paying themself. Say it's a six-month engagement, I say, "We get the money out of the way, then I'm all-in, and you're all-in for six months at which point we will reset our engagement goals and you can decide to continue for another six months."

HOW MUCH TO CHARGE

You have been patiently waiting to know how much to charge. Let's go through the most common mistakes I have seen coaches make with pricing:

1. Self-worth. We talked about this above, but it is worth mentioning as a mistake. "After all, I do have an MBA, and twenty years of corporate experience, that must be worth something." Yes, it's valuable, but this is a business transaction and a supply-and-demand question.
2. Market pricing. "Well, coaches in my area, with my experience, are charging $400 per hour, I should charge at least

that." OK. How many clients do you have? Are you as busy as you want to be?

3. Not charging enough and not being able to keep up with the demand.
4. Charging too much, such as having more time to offer than what people are willing to pay for because your price is too high.
5. If you think about the "value" of the coaching sessions, not every session is necessarily worth $1,000 but twenty sessions can be worth more than $20,000. The journey to unlimited possibilities is priceless.

SUPPLY VERSUS DEMAND

Allow me to share a simple economics theory for price optimization. Let's say you have ten apples to sell and you price them at $1 each and you have twenty people wanting to buy them at that price. $1 is probably not the optimal price then because you have many more people wanting apples at that price than you have apples to sell.

So, you change the price to $1.50 and now you have fifteen people willing to pay $1.50 for an apple. The following week when you get your shipment, you price them at $2 each. Now you have ten people willing to pay $2 so your supply of ten apples meets the demand of ten apples.

You get a bit cocky, and you decide to price your apples at $3 each with the next shipment. Now you have four people willing to pay $3 an apple and you have six apples that go to waste. You can imagine there are many more inputs we could play with here including discounting the last six apples the day before they rot but we're not doing that with coaching.

There is an argument for creating scarcity like pricing them a little under $2 so you always have a couple of people who just couldn't get an apple so they will line up earlier for one next week and others will then see how valuable your apples are and will tell their friends to come early for them, and so on. Eventually you will be able to charge $4 an apple but now we're getting into marketing and messaging.

Let's bring this back to coaching. First let's determine your supply. If you recall, in Chapter 4 we talked about how many clients a week you can coach while being able to do the pre and post work thoroughly and grow your business? Let's say that the number of clients is twenty. Let's assume you meet them weekly, which means your supply is then twenty sessions per week. The exercise now is to figure out what price will fill those twenty spots.

For ease of numbers, let's say you decided that your three-month program will be priced at $3,000 for ten sessions. Yes, there are thirteen weeks in three months, but the coach and client need some room for travel, etcetera, so a three-month program of ten sessions is a good place to start. In this case, if you are already established and experienced as a coach, I would not recommend any less than a six-month engagement which would then be $6,000. There are more variables here and different services you can offer within the engagement but let's keep the math simple for now.

You are offering ten sessions at $3,000. The question is how long will it take you to fill twenty spots at that price? I am only focused on price here, not the other components of business development which I will get into shortly.

If there is too much resistance at this price, then you need to start lower and increase. If there is too much demand at this price and you have tons of people waiting to work with you, then you are not charging enough. You are looking for that sweet spot which creates a bit of tension on pricing where people aren't fighting over the apples, but that makes sure all your apples are sold. One coach I met with priced their session at $250/hour when the market range for her service was probably in the $100-400 range. She struggled to get her first few clients. If she had priced at $100, she could have instantly had ten clients try it out and within weeks of getting busy, she would have created demand for her supply. She would then have people talking about how good she is and referring their friends, slowly raising her price to $250 without interrupting the demand.

Whatever price you are at, it is temporary. I can share with you that I signed up thirty clients within weeks to work with me at $3,600 for ten sessions. I increased that price within a year to $10,000 for six months. At the time I am writing this book, I charge $50,000 for a six-month engagement. The only thing I focus on is whether all the slots I offer are filled and if there's a bit of tension at that price.

INCOMING

Marketing, branding, social media, etcetera are huge topics worthy of at least one other book. Until now, we have focused on matching supply and demand for optimal pricing. For the sake of our conversation here I just want to bring your awareness to the different components that can increase the demand, which can also ultimately increase your price if your supply stays the same. Now you can increase your supply by adding members to your team at different prices, and that is also a different aspect of business growth.

For now, as the words are self-explanatory, it's worth considering the components of the business growth process:

- **Lead Generation**: Where do your leads come from and what systems are you creating and using to generate more leads?
- **Lead Nurturing**: Once you have a lead, how do you nurture the lead, stay in touch, add value, and grow the connection with the lead so that you are top of mind when it comes time to choose a coach.
- **Conversion**: Your lead is now ready to make a decision. Do you have the skills and processes to convert this coaching prospect into a coaching client?
- **Delivery**: Your prospect became a client. They are now in a program. How do they rate your service, your relationship, your process? Are they seeing results from the coaching program? Are you delivering everything they expected and more? Will they give you rave reviews?
- **Upsell**: Your client completed their program. Do you let them float out the

door or do you have a clear sense of how to get them to the next level? Are you able to explain how more time with you will drive more results? Is your renewal process a no-brainer?

Remember my client Alex with the WIIFM? He told me he had recently been turned down for some projects and asked me what I thought went wrong.

> Alex: "I had a couple of projects opportunities fall through recently and I'm not sure why. I'm tempted to just say you win some you lose some."

> Me: "Knowing your level of talent, I would not say you need to lose any. At the same time, if you are winning every pitch, you are probably not asking for enough business. We can look at your pitch and how you ask for the order. However, there are five stages of the sales cycle and if your pitch did not win the business, then you want to go upstream and ask how you had nurtured your lead. The warmer the nurturing, the less effort needed at the conversion. Then you go further upstream and ask what

branding and messaging they received upon first contact."

You can go even further back if there was a referral involved and ask yourself how well you upsell your current clients so that they are also selling future clients for you. Most importantly, was the referring client so pleased with the delivery that just sharing their experience with their friend pre-sold the lead? Understand the journey of your prospect from first point of contact to being a client for a lifetime.

BUSINESS IS PERSONAL

This is a people business and the more you open your heart the greater a contribution you will be to the lives and success of others. This business is personal. And it is also a business. You are coaching others to succeed in all their endeavors and with these tools, you can be very successful in your own.

In this chapter you have worked through some of your own attachments to money and what role it has played in your life and raised your awareness of what role this relationship plays in your business. You have learned a formula that separates your self-worth from how you price your services to maintain a balanced energy exchange between you and your clients. You have learned how to connect with and convert a client during a chemistry session. You have also learned what questions to ask yourself if you just don't feel masterful at business development. It can happen. These are growth cycles for your business and for yourself.

Everything is here for you. Money and love are not exclusive. Approach this business with a big heart, and an objective mind, and you will create magic.

SHARPEN YOUR TOOLS

"What did you know?" I asked Michelle. I could see her wheels turning. "What did you know that you were pretending not to know?" At the same time, her mind was going "Huh? What does that even mean?" Her body language shifted, and she settled in a little more and softly smiled. So much of our work is nonverbal yet we focus mostly on what we say and what they say. The question came from my gut. I felt what I was saying and where I wanted to guide her to. The fact that I got past her super sharp brain was cool. Michelle may not have been completely aware of this but the last few months, my goal was to empower her with her knowing. She was already extremely knowledgeable and successful. She was always an amazing student, and she could jump into a new business or new function and master it in no time. What she wasn't as aware of was just how powerful her instincts and intuition were. For example, she was telling me about a successful hire she had made and justified the success by telling me about how this person's experience and skills were a fit for the job. I reminded her the person who left the role had a similar profile. I knew it was more than that. Michelle is a powerful being, more powerful than she's ever known herself to be. She's very experienced and knowledgeable but her true power comes from her inner knowing, even more than her knowledge. Her knowing may direct her to acquire the knowledge to support, justify, and validate what she already knows intuitively but the original source is deeper.

The reason I know this is because I am constantly learning and integrating new tools and techniques into my practice. Everything I learn benefits my clients. Every personal development process I embrace opens doors for my clients. This is part of my mission motivation. Knowing my growth helps others grow with more ease, keeps me evolving. When Michelle asked me where I had been the prior week, I said I was out for a week of training, and you could see I peaked her interest. I had been coaching her for eight years and I always brought newness to our work together. We have worked together through many of her personal and professional transitions, and she knows how the system works. We grow together.

TOOLS, TOOLS, AND MORE TOOLS

Over the past thirteen years I have integrated so many tools into my special sauce. As coaches, most of us start with whatever coaching education we choose, which in my case was IPEC. We add to that our career experience, or personal experience, or both. Over time, as you keep learning, it all layers in to create something unique. Many years ago, I added the Hogan Leadership Assessment and made sure our team was the best at it by hiring a Hogan trainer to meet with us every week for five years until we knew it inside out. We still have a Hogan trainer on our team, as well as a former IPEC trainer. I also became a Theta Healing practitioner, which I was initially doing for my benefit but what I learned about limiting beliefs and how they create our life experiences unconsciously was mind-blowing. Theta also taught me a way to change those beliefs, thereby creating change in my world.

Inspired by Tony Robbins and how fluid he is with the use of NLP, we brought in an NLP trainer and got the whole team trained. I have been a student of Kabbalah for over fifteen years, so I would bring my teacher Benjamin in to meet with the team every week to inspire us to do our spiritual work not only for our benefit but mostly for the benefit of our clients.

Then I learned about Dr. Joe Dispenza and started meditating over an hour a day and integrating his points of view, much in line with my spiritual background that parallel universes exist where there are no problems, only possibilities. We can create a space through meditation where we tap into and create different "realities" in our lives.

More recently, I have been inspired by the teachings and practices of Access Consciousness which is consistent with everything I know to be true, that our point of view (conscious or unconscious) creates our reality, and our work is to remain in the question to stay in the flow.

This is in addition to the hundreds of podcasts I listen to, YouTube videos I watch, and books I read to keep expanding my awareness and my skills as a coach.

I share all my secrets with you here and most of my clients would be surprised to read all this because I don't sell any of this to them. By stepping into my greatness more and more each day of my life, I bring them into a Space of infinite possibilities without using the lingo. I meet them with their language, not the language of these other practices. At the end of the day, I'm still just coaching them. We are talking about work, about leadership, about growing business, leading teams, emotional intelligence, executive presence, meeting deadlines, conflict resolution, overcoming stress and challenges. We are working on the stuff that feels "normal" to them, but what we are doing is changing their norms, shifting the paradigms from conclusion to possibilities, and from limitations to choices.

I hold Space, I care for them, I am curious, I acknowledge and validate their experience, and I ask open-ended questions to expand their horizons and awareness so they can be empowered to lead themselves to the infinite possibilities.

Everything I learn and how I grow shows up in their sessions and eases the way to their growth. It's just amazing when something I just watched pops into our session and affects my client. They didn't even have to watch the five-part Brené Brown series about emotions on the flight with me the day before.

TRAINING

Almost 50 percent of coaches reported increasing time spent receiving training during the pandemic. Isn't that amazing? As soon as they had more time on their hands, every other coach took advantage of that by taking their medicine and learning and developing. These are the coaches you want to be working with. These are the coaches you want to *be*, and more. Do not worry so much about how it all comes together. Keep learning and experiencing and when you take the time to allow it to come together, you will create something new and exciting for you and your clients. When you are excited about growth, you will inspire others to grow. Have I driven the message home yet that we are all connected?

Create a learning calendar for yourself. Will you get trained or certified in a new approach this year? What books will you read this month? Which podcasts are you listening to? I remember when Sindy was a member of our team, she told me she had a goal to read one leadership book and one fun book every month and by the end of the year she had read at least twenty-four books and had learned a lot she could integrate in her coaching practice and also had also allowed her mind to travel into many fictional worlds.

You are setting a pace for other people in this world. As you pick up speed, you will see the world around you change more quickly. As you slow down, so will your environment. There is a time for everything, and sometimes we need to slow down to speed up. Have fun, keep learning, keep it light, and keep expanding your awareness.

12

IS THIS FOR YOU?

If you want to be a guru, or an advisor, or a subject-matter expert, this process is not for you. Coaching is not problem-solving, even though we have all experienced rewards from being problem solvers. Just because you can solve somebody's problem, does not mean you should.

This is only for coaches who are willing to be all-in and take responsibility for co-creating endless possibilities for people. This is not for coaches who want to give answers. It's for curious, caring, and committed coaches who are willing to show up for others completely and be the change they want to see in others.

This process is also not for coaches who have a Plan B – "If this doesn't work out, I'll just go get a job or work for the family business." If you are waiting for this business to prove to you that you can be a coach, then you have it upside down. You are a coach. If you had nothing to prove today, what would you create? You are the Creator.

As I was writing the final chapters of this book, I got a call from a coach who had launched his business two years ago, and like many examples in this book, had not yet hit his stride. He was doing some work for his alma mater, he had done a couple of pilot programs with small corporates that did not extend, and he was doing some volunteer work. These were all great places to start. I asked what he thought was getting in his way and he said, "Too many ideas." I took a quick look at his Hogan Leadership Assessment, and it told me otherwise. It told me that when he was under stress and the self-doubt crept in then he changed his mind to try and see if something else would work better. I could also see that he was sensitive to what others thought of him and was waiting for recognition that he had been successful. I assured him we *all* go through this. None of it was particularly new to me from what I had seen. He had not yet found the tipping point where his mission motivation was steam-rolling the self-doubt and "what will people think." I told him I was writing a book for him.

This is for coaches who are willing to look in the mirror and ask themselves the questions:

- How am I contributing energy to this client's situation? For better or for worse? Am I in the box with them? Am I buying their stories? Do I have the same stories myself?
- Who can I *be* and what can I *do* differently to create the space, possibilities, choices, and contribution for this person to experience success and fulfillment beyond their wildest dreams? If I wasn't trying to be liked by my client, what would I do differently?
- How willing am I to take responsibility and do my own work to pave the way for others?

Do not rob them of their opportunity to choose. Do not take away their free will. Think of a toddler learning to walk. I remember one day my daughter suddenly realized she could walk. We were about ten blocks from home in New York City. She could only take a few steps at a time, so we were not really ready to let her out of the stroller to get us all the way home. She was not having it. She insisted on walking, even though she was wearing sock-like shoes. She refused to have her hand held and she walked the entire ten blocks, five steps at a time, stopping to wave at everyone with a big smile. The pleasure and pride she had from taking her steps on her own was worth everything, including the hour it took to get home.

You can co-create so much magic. Every step you take will teach someone else to walk taller, stronger, and happier. Go for it. Smile and wave.

13

DREAM COME TRUE

It was an unusually warm January day. It got as high as sixty-five that day but by the time Ted came over at 5:00 p.m., it was already dark and a bit chillier. We decided to light the fire pit outside and sat around for what turned out to be a meaningful two-hour conversation for both of us. I had planned to share all my secrets of success with Ted since I could sense his passion and enthusiasm as a new coach. Ted had come to me about a year prior with curiosity about coaching and I had whetted his appetite enough for him to immediately sign up for his coaching certification. He meant business.

I've guided dozens of coaches over the years to decide whether this role or this business is right for them, to figure out what's working or not in their current practice, and in many cases, to accelerate their process to not only playing a crucial role in the success of others, but also creating a sustainable business for themselves. As you now know, if you can't crack your own success formula, you won't even be around to help others crack theirs.

As with the first time we met, Ted was eager, and diligently absorbed as much as he could, as we simplified his model and gave him the confidence he needed to resign shortly thereafter. Why am I telling you about Ted? Well, Ted and all the other Teds out there are the reason I wrote this book. What started off as me mentoring him, turned out to be a gift for me as I remembered just how excited I get talking and teaching about coaching. You see, I've been successful at many things in life, but none have provided as much joy and pleasure as impacting the success of others. Nothing gives the level of fulfillment and satisfaction as knowing I activated something in someone else that makes them want to do the same for others. And so on. And so on.

Ted wanted to know what mistakes I had made, and what regrets I had. He wanted to know how many revenue sources he should have, he wanted to know where to not waste his time, he wanted to know what to charge, when to start, and with whom. Like me, he also wanted to know how to help people who couldn't afford executive coaching yet he still felt compelled to contribute to. Like many of us, Ted had questions about how to be in service for others yet make tons of money as well. Sometimes coaches believe those are mutually exclusive. They are certainly not. In fact, they can't exist separately. If you can't make money, you won't be around to help people. If you're not in this with your heart, you won't make enough money for a sustainable future. They go together.

Every time Ted asked me a question, I not only had the answer that would save him tons of time and effort, I also had tons of examples to show how and why it worked. I had a story to support every scenario. It was so much fun and there was no way I could fit it into the time we had together. I had already committed to writing this book, so I kept saying "Oh, yes. I'll have to include that in my book, and you'll read all about it."

There's a lot of leverage in this business. If I have an idea and I go out and try ten different ways to execute on it, I'm going to end up with at least one or two ways that work, and a couple of runner ups. If Ted grabs four of my ten, tries them and succeeds at one or two and adds one of his own, then the next person who asks him will save even more time and effort and try two of Ted's, add one of his own, and on we go. Why is that leverage for me? I want to change the way we work. I want to change the way we communicate. I want to change the way we bring our entire being to work. I am physically limited by my calendar but energetically infinite by passing down the wisdom. I'm happy to be part of the energy pyramid, knowing everything I contribute to someone else's life has the potential to impact an endless number of people. Sometimes you help a stranger in the subway just with a kind smile because you just walked out of a coaching session where your coach helped redirect your frustration into an opportunity.

Things can change for you, and they can change in an instant. If I spent 10,000 hours coaching and you can receive the energy of that from me, and apply some tools that work for you, you can get the results of 10,001 hours of coaching with a single hour. Try it. Be a co-creator. Know that what's coming *through* you rather than *from* you is what's helping people. Not just your brains or your work ethic. That's an old model that has served its time. It's not an hour of work for an hour of results anymore. Surround yourself with inspiring people, create a disciplined model and approach that works for you, then know you are standing on the shoulders of giants that came before you and the outcomes will be exponential. If Tony Robbins hadn't done what he did, I wouldn't be here. He, amongst others, opened the vault for us. Now we know what's possible. We know what an intervention means, and we know that you don't need weeks and months to shift someone. If he hadn't gone through what he did personally, professionally, financially, it still would've been hard for us. But it's not. Trust me. If you do everything I've said in this book, you will be amazed with yourself.

I wrote this book for you. I wrote this book because the quicker I can help you align with your soul's purpose, the quicker we will lead millions of people to their greatness. Clearly you are here to help others succeed and let all the magic flow through your life as well in the process. What else is truly possible for you now? What did you know to even pick up this book? What little voice spoke to you and said, "I know I can, I know I can, I know I can." You got this. This is who you are not just what you do. How much more love can you give? How much more fun can you have? This is winning.

ACKNOWLEDGMENTS

I have wanted to write this book for a long time, to share the secrets of my success, and it was not until a good chat with my dear friend Angela Lauria that it became a reality. This book would not have gotten into your hands without Angela and her phenomenal team at Difference Press. Angela, and my editor Cory Hott, not only have the brilliance and expertise for such a creation, they also had the warmth, kindness, and determination to support me through all stages of the writing process, including the emotional ones.

I want to thank Paul and our children, Zahara, and Zed, who get so excited about my books. I imagine my kids reading about me and my passion for coaching for a long time to come and it warms my heart. Thank you for your kindness, unconditional love, your curiosity, and sincerity. You inspire me to become a better and better version of myself every day. I love you both so much.

Thank you to my many teachers at the Kabbalah center who have directly and indirectly inspired me and encouraged me to find my way of spreading consciousness to reduce pain, suffering, and chaos in the world. You have taught me to love, and to receive love, and to seek my personal growth courageously. You also always remind me that no matter how far we have come, the possibilities are endless and our impact on the world is infinite. Thank you. I love you.

Special thanks to my parents, Dad, Mom, and Izzy. You have taught me persistence and determination. I have learned from you to never give up, never give in, and never quit. Thank you. I love you.

To my first-grade teacher, Mrs. Sylvia Kerman. I have been thinking about you a lot these past few years and wish I could have told you myself what an impact you made on my life, even now, almost fifty years later. You saw me. And you knew exactly what I needed to know about myself. I still recall overhearing you talking to my mom and feeling so special and capable. Thank you. I love you.

Finally, thank you to my clients and my readers. You are the reason I do what I do, and I constantly strive to better myself as a coach. You give me courage to keep evolving. Your passions for your career and your desire to bring all of yourself into the workplace inspire me daily. We are in this together, and the world is becoming a better place because of it.

ABOUT THE AUTHOR

Tanya Ezekiel is the CEO of Conductive Coaching, a thriving executive coaching and team development firm based in New York City. She and her team of coaches take ambitious executives to new heights leading them to become effective leaders and happier human beings all-around. Tanya believes deeply in the coaching connection and relationship as the main ingredient to success. Through her commitment and care to the relationship and process of transformation, she designs a space for awareness and co-creation of infinite possibilities, thus activating the potential inside each one of us.

Following a successful career on Wall Street as a bond trader and managing director, Tanya followed her knowing to become a guide and contributor to other peoples' success. She became certified as a coach at IPEC (Institute for Professional Excellence in Coaching) and launched her company in 2010 in midtown Manhattan. Leveraging her broad network in financial services, she became a whisperer to C-suite executives and beyond. Her first bestseller, *Activate Your Opportunities: The Change Agent's Guide to More Impact with Less Stress,* was a hit amongst leaders looking to up-level their contribution.

Tanya believes that in order to be a conduit of energy to inspire others, we must have a profound understanding of our own operating system, and how to constantly upgrade and finetune our model to achieve and maintain flow. She is spiritually hungry, practicing a deep study of ancient wisdom to access higher levels of consciousness, as well as meditation, and breathwork. She is an avid and adventurous learner, with a nonstop desire to learn, teach, and coach others to expand what's possible for them.

Tanya earned her bachelor's degree in finance and international business from McGill University and her MBA at Cornell University. She lives in Brooklyn with her young children, Zahara and Zed.

ABOUT DIFFERENCE PRESS

Difference Press is the publishing arm of The Author Incubator, an Inc. 500 award-winning company that helps business owners and executives grow their brand, establish thought leadership, and get customers, clients, and highly-paid speaking opportunities, through writing and publishing books.

While traditional publishers require that you already have a large following to guarantee they make money from sales to your existing list, our approach is focused on using a book to grow your following – even if you currently don't have a following. This is why we charge an up-front fee but never take a percentage of revenue you earn from your book.

☞ MORE THAN A COACH. MORE THAN A PUBLISHER. ✍

We work intimately and personally with each of our authors to develop a revenue-generating strategy for the book. By using a Lean Startup style methodology, we guarantee the book's success before we even start writing. We provide all the technical support authors need with editing, design, marketing, and publishing, the emotional support you would get from a book coach to help you manage anxiety and time constraints, and we serve as a strategic thought partner engineering the book for success.

The Author Incubator has helped almost 2,000 entrepreneurs write, publish, and promote their non-fiction books. Our authors have used their books to gain international media exposure, build a brand and marketing following, get lucrative speaking engagements, raise awareness of their product or service, and attract clients and customers.

☞ ARE YOU READY TO WRITE A BOOK? ✎

As a client, we will work with you to make sure your book gets done right and that it gets done quickly. The Author Incubator provides one-stop for strategic book consultation, author coaching to manage writer's block and anxiety, full-service professional editing, design, and self-publishing services, and book marketing and launch campaigns. We sell this as one package so our clients are not slowed down with contradictory advice. We have a 99 percent success rate with nearly all of our clients completing their books, publishing them, and reaching bestseller status upon launch.

☞ APPLY NOW AND BE OUR NEXT SUCCESS STORY ✍

To find out if there is a significant ROI for you to write a book, get on our calendar by completing an application at www.TheAuthorIncubator.com/apply.

OTHER BOOKS BY DIFFERENCE PRESS

Power Your Pay: The All-In Female Entrepreneur's Guide to Make Millions and Still Be Yourself by Delaine Blazek

Give Your Kids Financial Freedom: A Simple, Step-by-Step System to Securing Your Children's Future by Roger Bryan

Simple Healthy Habits: A Guide to Achieving Optimal Mental and Physical Wellness by Jannette L. Corpus

Take Back Your Dreams: Prioritize Your Purpose, Regain Control of Your Time, and Create the Life You Want Before It's Too Late by Sandy Dempsey

From Overwhelmed to Optimized: Reignite Your Purpose, Reclaim Your Resilience, and Rejuvenate Your Nonprofit Career by Janie Ginocchio

I'm Divorced, Now What?: The Strong Woman's Guide to Your New Life as a Single Mom by Izibeloko O. Jack-Ide

The Master Plant Experience: The Science, Safety, and Sacred Ceremony of Psychedelics by Maya Shetreat, MD

Human Design and Essential Oils: The Facilitator's Guide to Using Plant Prana to Align with Your Type, Strategy, Authority, Profile, and Centers by Robin Winn, MFT & Greg Toews

THANK YOU!

Listen, Coach. I'm fully aware that reading a book can take time – something you probably don't have a lot of. For that, know that I am grateful. You're taking the first step to improving your coaching skills and helping your clients get the results they deserve. We need more people like you to make the world a better place.

As a token of my gratitude, I want to help you take this training one step further by offering you this link to a free twenty-minute webinar to get started with the next steps to your future success as a coach at www.ConductiveCoaching.com/gift

You can also check out some short and impactful videos at www.YouTube.com/@conductive1286/videos

Many thanks,
Tanya

Made in United States
North Haven, CT
19 January 2025